The Final Rollercoaster

When Elijah and Jezebel Ride Again

DESMOND FORD

iUniverse, Inc.

Bloomington

The Final Rollercoaster:

When Elijah and Jezebel Ride Again

iUniverse books may be ordered through booksellers or by contacting:

iUniverse
1663 Liberty Drive
Bloomington, IN 47403
www.iuniverse.com
1-800-Authors (1-800-288-4677)

ISBN: 978-1-4502-6598-0 (pbk)
ISBN: 978-1-4502-6601-7 (ebk)

Printed in the United States of America
iUniverse rev. date: 11/30/10

Chapters

Special Thanks

To Carol Smith and Coral Cherry
who both helped with proofing this manuscript.

Preface

In the beginning there was chaos, and the earth was without form and void. Then God began his mighty acts of creation. First, the Spirit of God moved upon the waters. Second, God spoke the world into existence (Gen 3-26; 29-30). The symbol of the Spirit moving on the waters in Genesis 1 will be used in many places in Scripture to announce and define God's mighty acts of redemption.

At the time of Noah's Flood, God decides to destroy the earth because of wholesale corruption (Gen 6-8). Noah, figure of Christ, is alone seen as righteous. According to God's command, Noah builds the ark to house the believers. Salvation of the righteous and judgment on the wicked occur simultaneously, and the wicked, attacking the ark, perish in the flooding waters.

Later in Scripture "flooding waters" become a symbol of evil hordes of people who attack the saints.

Then God dries up the flood by sending a wind over the earth, and the waters recede (Gen 8:1-5). Here the creation imagery of the Spirit moving on the waters becomes the wind dividing and drying up the flooding waters.

During the Exodus, God tells Moses:

> Tell the Israelites to move on. Raise your staff and stretch out your hand over the sea to divide the water so that the Israelites can go through the sea on dry ground.

Ex 14:15,16

> Then Moses stretched out his hand over the sea, and all that night the LORD drove the sea back with a strong east wind and turned it into dry land. The waters were divided.

Ex 14:21

Here Scripture again uses creation imagery of the Spirit of God ("spirit" again equals "wind"—they are the same word in the original) to divide and dry up the waters.

The same act that brings redemption of God's people from their captivity in Egypt, leads to the destruction of their enemies. The "new creation" is of Israel as a nation.

Hence in Scripture redemption is repeatedly viewed and expressed as a new creation—of both groups and individuals. For the latter, see 2 Corinthians 5:17: "Therefore, if anyone is in Christ, he is a new creation; the old has gone, the new has come!"

Another application of the drying up of the waters is found during the Babylonian Captivity. In Daniel chapter 5 we read of King Belshazzar and his great feast. Judgment is announced, and the words "Mene, mene, tekel, upharsin" are written on the wall (Dan 5:25-28). King Cyrus who, like Christ at his Second Coming, arrives from the East. He diverts the river Euphrates, thus drying up the riverbed that surrounded and protected the city, and enters by stealth (Jer 51:36-40, passages in Isaiah, and various historical sources).

Here a redeemer, a figure of Christ, dries up the waters and redeems God's people from captivity. At the same time the enemies of God are despatched.

When we move to the New Testament, the book of John begins, as does Genesis, with the words "In the beginning." John is here announcing the coming of Jesus in creation imagery. Here is the creation of the Last Adam:

> Therefore, just as sin entered the world through one man, and death through sin, and in this way death came to all men, because all sinned …
>
> Rom 5:12
>
> But the gift is not like the trespass. For if the many died by the trespass of the one man, how much more did God's grace and the gift that came by the grace of the one man, Jesus Christ, overflow to the many! Again, the gift of God is not like the result of the one man's sin: The judgment followed one sin and brought condemnation, but the gift followed many trespasses and brought justification. For if, by the trespass of the one man, death reigned through that one man, how much more will those who receive God's abundant provision of grace and of the gift of righteousness reign in life through the one man, Jesus Christ.
>
> <u>Consequently, just as the result of one trespass was condemnation for all men, so also the result of one act of righteousness was justification that brings life for all men.</u> For just as through the disobedience of the one man the many

were made sinners, so also through the obedience of the one man the many will be made righteous.

Rom 5:15-19

So it is written: "The first man **Adam** became a living being"; the **last Adam**, a life-giving spirit.

1 Cor 15:45

When John baptizes Jesus, he uses creation imagery to describe the coming of the Redeemer. Again creation and salvation are linked. John declares, "I saw the Spirit come down from heaven as a dove and remain on him." The dove represents the Holy Spirit fluttering over Jesus as he is baptized, dividing the waters (Jn 1:29-34). Here is the re-expression of the imagery of Genesis chapter one where the Spirit "moved" over the waters, as the dove "fluttered" or "hovered" over Christ.

In Matthew chapter 8 and two other Gospels we read of the episode where Jesus calms the troubled waters.

Then he got into the boat and his disciples followed him. Without warning, a furious storm came up on the lake, so that the waves swept over the boat. But Jesus was sleeping. The disciples went and woke him, saying, "Lord, save us! We're going to drown!"

He replied, "You of little faith, why are you so afraid?" Then he got up and rebuked the winds and the waves, and it was completely calm.

Mt 8:23-27

Christ's words subdue the tumultuous waters, which shows the inseparable liaison between the work of the Holy Spirit and the words of Christ, as in Genesis 1:2,3.

In these examples, we have seen symbols of the Spirit used and re-used in the Scriptures to describe the creation imagery used in God's redemptive acts. In summary, we've seen the Spirit's work described as 1. the Spirit Himself (Gen 1); 2. the wind (the Flood and the Exodus), 3. the acts of a righteous man, Cyrus (Babylonian Captivity), 4. a dove (Christ's baptism); 5. Christ's word (the calming of the storm).

The wind, the breath, the dove are known as symbols for the Spirit of God who acts along with God's spoken and written Word. Again, creation symbols are used repeatedly in the Bible to announce and describe God's redemptive acts.

And now, with Elijah at Mount Carmel, in contest with the priests of Baal, we see the same imagery used. King Ahab of Israel, led by his wife Jezebel, was a Baal worshiper. They had killed many of Israel's true prophets, and only righteous Elijah and a faithful 7,000 were left. Despite Jezebel and Ahab who are intent on his death (1 Kings 18:4-13), Elijah faces up to Ahab and commands him to summon the people of Israel to Mount Carmel (1 Kings 18:19).

At Mount Carmel's base rose the River Kishon, which flowed into the Valley of Megiddo. Megiddo was the historical site of many of Israel's battles with her enemies. Megiddo becomes a symbol for Armageddon in the Book of Revelation, the symbol of the final battle between good and evil. The River Euphrates is used as a symbol of flooding waters in the OT books and the Book of Revelation.

Louis Were noted this long ago:

> Thus we see that the employment in Rev. 16:12 of the
> waters of the Euphrates as the symbol of the "peoples, and
> multitudes, and nations, and tongues" who, under Babylonian
> instruction, seek to overwhelm the people of God in the final

struggle between the forces of good and evil is that which is the *normal* application running throughout all the Scripture

The Certainty of the Third Angel's Message, p. 236

Let's go back to the contest at Mount Carmel, where Elijah utters a challenge to the people:

> "How long will you waver between two opinions? If the Lord is God, follow him; but if Baal is God, follow him."

> 1 Kings 18:21

Note Elijah's courage. He is the only one of the Lord's prophets left and Baal, a pagan god, has 450 prophets, and Jezebel another 400 (1 Kings 18:19). Elijah gives instructions: "Get two bulls, let them choose theirs, kill them and cut them into pieces and put them on the wood" (1 Kings 18:22-23). Elijah adds, "but do not set fire to it."

He sets the rules: "Then you call on the name of your god, and I will call on the name of the LORD. The God who answers by fire—he is God"(1 Kings 18:24).

The people agree to this, and the prophets of Baal get busy sacrificing their bull and setting up the altar. These false prophets call on the name of Baal morning to noon, dancing around the altar.

Elijah begins to taunt them at noon. "'Shout louder!' Surely he is a god! Perhaps he is deep in thought, or busy, or travelling. Maybe he is sleeping and must be awakened" (1 Kings 18:26-27). The false prophets slash themselves with swords and spears, ... until their blood flows (1 Kings 18:28). They continue until the time for the evening sacrifice.

Then Elijah calls the people to him. He repairs the altar, takes 12 stones to represent the tribes of Israel, and makes an altar. He digs a trench, arranges the wood, cuts the bull into pieces, and lays it on the wood. Then he fills four large jars with water and they pour it on the offering and wood. He repeats it twice, so that the water runs around the altar and even fills the trenches (1 Kings 18:30-35).

And then Elijah prays for God to act (1 Kings 18:36,37). Immediately, the fire of God falls and burns up the sacrifice, the wood, the stones and the soil, and also licks up the water in the trench (1 Kings 18:38). All see that the LORD is God. Then comes the destruction of the wicked in the area of Megiddo.

Again we see the creation imagery of God's spirit (here "fire") drying up the waters. Here the Creator God is again acting as Redeemer of his people and Judge of the wicked.

And now we see this story reapplied in the Book of Revelation:

> Then the angel said to me, "The waters you saw, where the prostitute sits, are peoples, multitudes, nations and languages. The beast and the ten horns you saw will hate the prostitute. They will bring her to ruin and leave her naked; they will eat her flesh and <u>burn her with fire</u>. For God has put it into their hearts to accomplish his purpose by agreeing to give the beast their power to rule, until God's words are fulfilled. The woman you saw is the great city that rules over the kings of the earth."

> Rev 17:15-18

Here in the final battle between good and evil, we see this creation/ redemption imagery used again. In Revelation 17:15-18, God by his Spirit puts it into the hearts of the wicked to burn the prostitute, Jezebel, who is sitting on the flooding waters. "The waters you saw, where the prostitute sits, are peoples, multitudes, nations and languages," vs. 15. The flooding water represents evil hordes that fight God and attack the saints. Here we have again the imagery from Mount Carmel of God's fire "drying up the waters." On the eve of their destruction the false prophets indulge the suicidal practice of gashing themselves with swords—judgment completes that process (Rev 17:16 and 1 Kings 18:40).

Elijah and Jezebel, in their antitype, are to ride again on the final rollercoaster of this earth's history. The story of Elijah, Ahab, and his evil wife Jezebel, is used in the Book of Revelation as a parable or symbol of what will happen at the end of time.

This OT story and its application to the Book of Revelation is the theme of this new work by Desmond Ford.

Note that fire is stronger than water. By its very nature, water extinguishes fire. You use water to put out fire, rarely the other way around. But here, God's fire is so powerful that—despite external appearances, despite the overwhelming flooding waters (evil multitudes)—FIRE OVERWHELMS WATER. This story allays our fears. The powers of evil are impotent. God has and will overcome them.

Here is a promise to encourage those who are new creatures in Christ:

> Place me like a seal over your heart, like a seal on your
> arm; for love is as strong as death; its jealousy unyielding as the
> grave.

> It burns like blazing fire, like a mighty flame.

Many waters cannot quench love, rivers cannot wash it away.

Song of Solomon 8:6-7

G. F.

Bible texts are NIV, except where mentioned or paraphrased.

Chapter One:

Elijah: Type of the End Time Saints

From a world where death seemed universal and invincible God took Enoch (of the patriarchal era) and Elijah (of the Jewish era). They entered Heaven without passing through the portals of the tomb. See Genesis 5:24 and 2 Kings 2:11. They prefigured the saints who will be translated without seeing death when Jesus returns (1 Thess 4:17). On the Mount of Transfiguration (Mt 17), Moses represented those who will rise from the grave, and Elijah those gathered from the living at the Second Advent.

This has long been understood, but it has not been as clearly seen that the whole career of Elijah, not just its end, has typical significance for believers at the end time. It is the purpose of this book to make that point clear.

Malachi's last words at the close of the Old Testament canon refer to Moses and Elijah and their significance for those living on the edge of "the great and dreadful day of the Lord." Practically all the early Church Fathers believed in the eschatological significance of this Old Testament farewell, and so have many scholars in recent centuries.

Others limit the application to the coming of John the Baptist who ministered "in the spirit and power of Elijah" (Lu 1:17). But Christ accepted both meanings as is clear in Matthew 17:11 12. "Elijah truly shall come and restore all things." The Baptist's day was hardly "the great and dreadful day of the Lord" in its ultimate meaning. The Baptist himself denied that he was Elijah. See John 1:20-23.

Almost all scholarly commentaries on Revelation have seen allusions to Moses and Elijah in Revelation 11:5,6. Moses had turned water to blood, and Elijah on several occasions prayed fire down from heaven. Revelation 11 is foretelling the ultimate destiny of those who oppose the "two witnesses" (the church as it proclaims the gospel at the end of time), as the miracles of Moses and Elijah similarly challenged those who opposed God's work through them. The early verses of Revelation 10 picture the fulfilment of Mark 13:10 and Matthew 24:14 and proclaim both the joy that comes to all who receive the gospel and the pain that subsequent persecution will inevitably bring. See Revelation 10:9-11. That persecution is predicted in the following chapter where Antichrist (the beast) makes war on the witnessing Church.

But there are other allusions in Revelation to the Old Testament story of Elijah. He ordered the death of the false prophets of Jezebel and they were destroyed in the region of Megiddo by the river Kishon. See 1 Kings 18:40 and compare Judges 5:19-21. Then consider the sevenfold reference to war in Revelation culminating in the war of Armageddon (16:16). See also 19:11-21.

Bishop Christopher Wordsworth gave us a splendid summary concerning Elijah in his famous commentary. We now append it:

> The name Elijah signifies "the Lord, Jehovah, He is God",
> and the life of Elijah agrees with his name. He came forward

as a faithful living witness, in an age of religious apostasy, to proclaim to idolatrous princes, priests, and people that the LORD he is God, and that he alone is God, and that all other gods are usurpers, and that their priests and prophets are to be exterminated from Israel according to God's law as guilty of rebellion against him (Deut 13:5; 18:20).

He came forth to bring Israel back to the true knowledge and worship of God, from which they had fallen to the service of Baal. He was a second Enoch. Enoch prophesied to the antediluvian world of Judgment to come (Jude 14), and pleased God, and was translated (Heb 11:5), without seeing death, as Elijah was.

Elijah was also another Moses, an asserter of the Divine Supremacy in opposition to the rival claims of heathen deities.

He was also a restorer of true religion. See Mal 4:6. … Elijah looked backward to Moses and to Enoch and he looked forward to Christ. He restored the Law and prepared the way for the Gospel. His miracles have both a retrospective and prospective character. In their sternness and severity against sin, as in the execution of God's vengeance against idolatry at Carmel and at Kishon, he awakened, as it were, the thunders and lightning of Horeb; but they also have evangelic gleams of mercy and love, as, for instance, in his tender care for the faithful widow of Zarephath. …

If the age in which Elijah had lived had been an ordinary time, this outburst and flashing forth of miraculous working in the dazzling splendour of his ministry would have been unaccountable.

But his position was altogether unprecedented; and the profusion of God's miraculous working in Elijah was due to the exorbitant wickedness of the rulers of Israel at that time, which required an extraordinary manifestation of God's divine power, asserting his supremacy, in order to recover his people from the ruin and misery into which they had fallen.

Elijah's life was a crisis in the history of Israel. Jeroboam had merged into Ahab; calf-worship had been developed into Baalism; the God of Israel had been supplanted by the idols of Phoenicia; the curse of Joshua on the builders of Jericho was defied; the thunders and lightnings of Sinai were forgotten; the Law of Moses was exploded; a Jezebel, the daughter of Ethbaal, the Priest of Baal, shared the Throne which had been occupied by David; and the abominations of Tyre and Sidon domineered in the capital of Israel.

The unique character of that age is exhibited by the Holy Spirit, not only in the Old Testament, but also in the New Testament. In the Apocalypse, when he would personify a corrupt Priesthood and Prophecy, he calls it a Jezebel (Rev 2:20); and when he would describe the working of those noble spirits who stand alone in a corrupt age, and fight against Antichristianism, he draws his imagery from the acts of Elijah (Rev 11:6).

...

Elijah was a forerunner of Christ. His first Advent was in the thick darkness of the worst days of Priestly degeneracy among the Jews, and in the thick gloom of heathen idolatry and unbelief. Then it was that the *Great Prophet,* whom Moses had pre-announced, was raised up to prophesy to the World

(Deut 18:18; Acts 3:22; 7:37). And it will be in a time of moral corruption in the world, and of spiritual degeneracy in a large part of Christian Israel, the Church of God, it will be in the hour of an Antichristian midnight; when his second Advent will shine like lightning from one part of heaven to the other (Matt 24:27; Lu 17:24.)

See *Wordsworth's Commentary on the Holy Bible*—1 Kings 18

The same learned commentator has some helpful comments on the last prophecy of the Old Testament, the one concerning the coming of Elijah the prophet. He lists many of the ancient Christian Church Fathers who imagined that Elijah would come in person before the Second Advent. But he also points out that, as the prophets call Christ David, because he is the true King and Shepherd of Israel, so the fulfilment of Malachi's prophecy does not require the return of the literal Elijah. It should be added that all local types and prophecies in the Old Testament, except of the Messiah, become worldwide in their New Testament application. Balaam, Jezebel, Babylon, Megiddo, Sodom, Gomorrah, Egypt's plagues, the beasts and horns of Daniel chapters 7 and 8, Israel's time of Jacob's trouble, the sealing or marking of God's people and their opposites, and the river Euphrates, etc., while local in the Old Testament, are all given a worldwide meaning in the New.

CHAPTER TWO:

JEZEBEL, THE ORIGINAL, AND HER WORLDWIDE ANTITYPE

The nemesis of Elijah was Jezebel, and, next to Christ, she is the most prominent figure in Revelation, being mentioned in the second chapter and then later in the book where two whole chapters are devoted to the system she represents—Babylon the Great, the Mother of harlots and abominations of the earth. See chapters 17 and 18. Like the typical Jezebel of the Old Testament, the wicked Babylon has a terrible end. Like her prototype, Babylon has been united to wicked government, which she has seduced and ruled. She, too, has slain the prophets of the Lord. Compare 1 Kings 18:13 and Revelation 18:20,24. As Jezebel is portrayed as delighting in lascivious garb, so it is with Babylon. Compare 2 Kings 9:30-37 and Revelation 17:4. When the final book of Scripture, one particularly dedicated to the last times, pictures a wicked entity at such considerable length—more than two chapters— it is clear we are meant to pay it special attention. And we who live in the nuclear age, when it has been demonstrated that the world is exceedingly vulnerable, will be wise if we give particular attention to what God has emphasized.

The story of Jezebel spans the closing chapters of l Kings beginning in chapter 16 and is climaxed in 2 Kings 9. She was a pagan princess dedicated to sun worship (see 2 Kings 23:5,6 and Ezekiel 8:12-16), and she led the king of Israel, who owed fealty to God, into the depths of heathen depravity. Through and through this "lady" is a monstrous killer set on wiping out all opposition to herself and her husband. By fraudulently attaching a false seal to a legal document she contrives to murder the innocent. See l Kings 21:8ff. (In Revelation 13 Antichrist has a false seal or mark for his law.) None of the worshipers of the true God are safe, and she condemns Elijah to death with a vicious oath. Being nervously and physically exhausted, the prophet of God is plunged into a blue funk.

This depression is referred to repeatedly in Scripture as pointing to the final time of tribulation for the true worshipers of the Creator. Jeremiah calls it "the time of Jacob's trouble," and it is part of the terrible tribulation mentioned by Daniel (12:1), referred to by Christ (Matt 24:21), and repeatedly alluded to in Revelation. See 3:10; 6:9-17; 7:14; 11:7-10; 12:17; 13:11-18; 14:20; 16:12-14; 17:13 and 19:19. But Elijah's depression is followed by translation to heaven, and so will it be with the saints living in the Last Days.

Other Old Testament prophets besides Daniel and Jeremiah symbolically portray the final onslaught on the people of God. See the last verses of Daniel 11, Joel 3:9-16, Zechariah 14, and Ezekiel chapters 38 and 39. This terrible time is typified in Jacob's night of wrestling (when fearful because of the approach of Esau with an armed band), and the tests over idolatry in Daniel chapters 1, 3, and 6. Particularly note that the key word in chapters 3 and 6 is "deliver" (KJV) and compare 12:1 where the same key word appears. The story of Esther, where genocide is threatened because of Israel's loyalty to the law of God, is yet another parallel.

Revelation repeatedly alludes to the false trinity of "the dragon, the beast, and the false prophet." See 12:3-13:1-12; 16:13; and 19:19-20:2. The dragon is a symbol of Satan (see 12:9); the beast is a counterfeit Messiah, a counterfeit Son of God, and the false prophet who brings fire down from heaven is the counterfeit Holy Spirit. Compare Acts 2 and Revelation 11:5.

The false prophet, the lamb with two horns, represents the leaders of Babylon's idolatrous hosts. He is first represented by a literary associate of Jezebel in Revelation 2:14—Balaam. Both Balaam and Jezebel signify those who tempt God's people into apostasy through spiritual fornication—false worship. See Numbers chapters 22, 24, and 31. Balaam, bribed by the King of Moab to curse Israel fails, but later he uses the heathen women of Moab to lead the men of Israel into fornication. It is this incident which lays the Scriptural foundation for its prediction of what the final Jezebel, Babylon the Great, will do in the end time.

Underlying all these crises is the first rebellion the universe ever witnessed, when Lucifer led many of the angelic hosts into apostasy. These fallen beings would become the demons so often referred to in the Gospels and again in the Bible's last book (Rev 9:14-21 and 16:13,14). Will beings made in their Creator's image worship their Maker only, or descend to the infernal spiritual depths of creature worship? That issue can be traced through both Old and New Testaments. Jezebel and Ahab imitate Lucifer by their idolatry, and the final conflict of earth will again be over the issue of choosing between the Creator and the great Apostate.

Because God likens his love relationship with his people to marriage, false worship is set forth as harlotry or fornication. See particularly Ezekiel chapters 16 and 23, chapters so terrible we would probably not read them aloud in public worship. There is nothing more repulsive to heaven than idolatrous worship—note the strong repelling language of these chapters.

CHAPTER THREE:

JEZEBEL'S STICKY END

Did God have no barrier against this trap of worshiping the creature instead of the Creator? Indeed He did. That barrier is repeatedly set forth as the divine obstacle to such apostasy. To that important matter we shall devote a later chapter in entirety.

So it is no careless image of Scripture when Jezebel is set forth as epitomizing false worship. Her Baal worship is considered by heaven as spiritual fornication. Again we would stress the fact that in devoting two whole chapters of Revelation to this issue (as well as many other verses), God is stressing the need for our attention and response lest we be beguiled.

It is no coincidence that when Israel was on the borders of the Promised Land she was led into fornication by Baal worshippers led by the false prophet Balaam. Thus we note the repetition of solemn warnings in Revelation 2 concerning those influenced by Balaam and Jezebel. When God's people are almost home many will be tragically seduced and fall from their fidelity like meteors of a shaken heaven. See Matthew 24:10-12; Revelation 6:12,13; and compare 1 Corinthians

10:5. Seeing this, we will understand why the letters to the seven churches in Revelation chapters two and three are not what we would have expected—portrayals of the pristine moral perfection of the early church. Instead, only two of the seven are without blame, the others wrestle with issues of false worship, and the final two are so nauseous that Christ is tempted to spit them out of his mouth. Please forgive our repetition of the point, but we are dealing now with eternal issues and the most dangerous seductive temptations ever experienced by the people of God. This book is no tract to fill in the time, but a shrill warning concerning your eternal destiny and mine.

Marvel at how wondrously the Bible is written. Here in the early books of Scripture we have in typical portrayals previews of the dangers of the church in all ages, but especially the last of the Last Days. It is our privilege to understand heaven's warnings and to spread the warnings abroad to a fallen world captivated by the allure of the worship of secularism.

We would also stress the fact that the Bible does not portray atheism as the last threat for Christ's church, but a false counterfeit religion. It is a two-horned beast like a lamb that leads the world to its final persecution of the saints. Babylon in Revelation is the name of a wicked woman, the counterfeit of the true church pictured in her radiant beauty in Revelation 12. (Note Jeremiah 6:2 and 2 Corinthians 11:2). Babylon is pictured astride the seven-headed beast, the emblem of governmental power that oppresses the church (Rev 17:1-7). Religion—false, idolatrous religion—will be the last resort of earth to soothe its troubles.

Ahab, the consort of Jezebel, the wicked king of rebellious Israel points to Babylon's consort at the end of time—the Antichrist. He is guided by the iniquitous counsels of his Queen, which lead him to murderous activities on a nationwide scale. But God is not sleeping, and eventually Ahab comes to his end with none to help him. 1 Kings 22:19-23 is of great importance.

> And he said, Hear thou therefore the word of the Lord: I saw the Lord sitting on his throne, and all the host of heaven standing by him on his right hand and on his left.

> And the Lord said, Who shall persuade Ahab, that he may go up and fall at Ramoth-Gilead? And one said on this manner, and another on that manner.

> And there came forth a spirit, and stood before the LORD, and said, I will persuade him.

> And the Lord said, Wherewith? And he said I will be a lying spirit in the mouth of all his prophets. And he said, Thou shalt persuade him, and prevail also: go forth, and do so.

> Now therefore, behold, the Lord hath put a lying spirit in the mouth of all these thy prophets, and the Lord hath spoken evil concerning thee.

Consider now Revelation 16:13 and 16:

> Then I saw three unclean spirits that looked like frogs; they came out of the mouth of the dragon, out of the mouth of the beast and out of the mouth of the false prophet. They are spirits of demons performing miraculous signs, and they go out to the kings of the whole world, to gather them for the battle on the great day of God Almighty. ...

> Then they gathered the kings together to the place that in Hebrew is called Armageddon.

King Ahab died in the battle that he had so eagerly anticipated. Thereby he typified the fate of the final Antichrist described in Revelation 14-20. And in a later chapter of 2 Kings we read of the awful fate of his wife—thrown from a high window, trampled underfoot by horses, and eaten by dogs. All this, despite her endeavors to charm her assailant Jehu, by "painting her eyes and arranging her hair." See 2 Kings 9:30-37. This fate took place in the valley of Jezreel, the valley of Megiddo, where her prophets had also died. Scripture repeatedly says that Ahab did worse than all before him, but it also says it was Jezebel who incited him to his evils. There is a distinct parallel between the biblical picture of the whore Babylon riding and controlling the nations (the seven-headed beast), and Jezebel's directing of Ahab. The destruction in the valley of Jezreel (Esdraelon—the valley of Megiddo) was an appropriate fate for the one who typified the final religious apostasy.

We must not miss the reference to Megiddo in Revelation 16:16. Armageddon signifies Mount of Slaughter and is made up of the Hebrew particle *Ha* for mountain and Megiddo, the well-known site of key battles in Israel's history. A mountain held up Jerusalem, and in Ezekiel 38 and 39 the latter day enemies of God's people perish on the mountains surrounding the Holy City.

Revelation 16:13 referred to the unclean spirits as "like frogs," and this is a reminder of Exodus 8:1-14. In the Exodus account we read that the pagan magicians of Pharaoh's kingdom counterfeited the divine miracles, but that after the counterfeit of the frogs they failed every time. Thus the seven last plagues on Egypt fell only on the Egyptians, while the Israelites were sheltered. Similarly, Revelation chapters 15, 16, and 18 make it plain that the world's seven last plagues are for the oppressors of God's people. In Revelation 18:4 God's people are called out of Babylon so as not to suffer the impending disasters.

Remember that Revelation 18:4 tells us that the plagues are Babylon's. They will wipe out the antitypical Jezebel and are the counterpart of the throwing down of the Zidonian princess and her terrible fate. And note that this judgment comes quickly upon her boasting of her power and impregnability. See 18:7.

There is no unanimity on the meaning of the name Jezebel, but Strong's *Concordance* links the main part of the name with the Hebrew word for "habitation." See lexicon 2083 and 2073. In John Farrar's work, *The Proper Names of the Bible*, published in 1855, the options given are: "island of the habitation, woe to the habitation, isle of the dunghill" (p. 137). In her commentary on Revelation, J. M. Ford tells us that the word translated "dwelling" or "habitation" in 18:2 only occurs here in the NT, but is found frequently in the Septuagint for the Jerusalem temple and for God's dwelling in heaven. But in 18:2 Babylon is the habitation of demons and of every unclean spirit.

We frequently disagree with dispensationalist J. A. Seiss, but his comments on Babylon are excellent and worthy of reproducing:

> The first thing which strikes me is … the evident
> correlation and contrast between the Woman here pictured,
> and another Woman described in the twelfth chapter. There,
> "a great sign was seen in the heaven, *a woman*"; here, it is
> remarked, "he bore me away in spirit into a wilderness, and
> I saw a *Woman*." Both these Women are mothers; the first:
> "brought forth a son, a male … who is to rule all the nations";
> the second "is the mother of harlots and of the abominations
> of the earth." Both are splendidly dressed; the first is "clothed

with the sun." Her raiment is light from heaven. The second is "clothed in purple and scarlet, decked with gold, and precious stones, and pearls." All her ornaments are from below, made up of things out of the earth and the sea.

Both are very influential in their position; the first has "the moon," the empress of night, the powers of darkness, "under her feet"; the second "hath rule, or kingdom, upon the kings of the earth." Both are sufferers; against the first is the Dragon, who stands watching to devour her child, and persecutes and pursues her, and drives her into the wilderness, and sends out a river to overwhelm her, and is at war with all her seed that he can find; against the second are the ten kings, who ultimately hate her, and make her desolate and naked, and eat her flesh, and burn her with fire, whilst God in his strength judges her, and visits her with plague, death, and utter destruction.

Both are very conspicuous and fill a large space in the history of the world, and in all the administrations of divine providence and judgment. That they are counterparts of each other there can hardly be a reasonable doubt. The one is a pure woman; the other is a harlot. The first is hated by the powers on earth; the second is loved, flattered, and caressed by them. Where the one has sway, things are heavenly; where the other lives, it is "wilderness." The one produces masculine nobility; which is ultimately caught away to God and to his throne; the other is supported and carried by the Dragon power—the beast with the seven heads and ten horns. The one has a diadem of twelve stars, wearing the patriarchs and apostles as her royal diadem; the other has upon her forehead the name of the greatest destroyer and oppressor of the holy people, and is drunken with "the blood of prophets and of saints, and of all that have been slain upon the earth."

The one finally comes out in a heavenly city, the New Jerusalem, made up of imperishable jewels, and arrayed in all the glory of God and the Lamb; the other finally comes out in a city of this world's superlative admiration, which suddenly goes down forever under the intense wrath of heaven, and becomes the habitation of demons, and a hold of every unclean spirit.

These two Women, thus related, and set over one against the other as opposites and rivals, must necessarily be interpreted in the same way. As Antichrist corresponds to Christ as a rival and antagonist of Christ, so Great Babylon corresponds to the Woman that bears the man-child, as *her* rival and antagonist.

By recalling, therefore, who and what is meant by the first Woman, we will be in a position to understand who and what is meant by the second.

Beyond question, the sun-clad Woman is God's great symbol of the visible Church—the Lamb's wife—the bone of His bone, and flesh of His flesh, fashioned out of His rifted side as the second Adam, who fell into a deep sleep of death for that purpose. ... What then can this rival Woman be but the organized Antichurch, the pseudo-church, the Bride made out of Satan, the universal body and congregation of false believers and false worshippers?

The Apocalypse, pp. 386-387

The many obvious parallels between Jezebel and Babylon are worthy of our consideration:

Meretricious [attracting attention in a vulgar manner]

Brazen

Murderous

Idolatrous and immoral

Accursed

Controls government

Defeated by Elijah

Counterfeits the king's laws using the pagan seal

Punished by God through human agents

The account of Jezebel and her husband with its references to the conflict between true and false worship, and the endeavour to kill God's spokesman Elijah, plus the slaughter of the false prophets and, ultimately, Jezebel in the Megiddo region leads us to now examine the antitype more closely.

CHAPTER FOUR:

THE CHURCH'S CALVARY

While Revelation chapters 1 to 11 concerns the church's experiences leading up to the end of time, the rest of the book revolves around the end itself. The time of trouble for God's witnesses and their martyrdom in chapter 11 are enlarged in the succeeding chapters. Revelation 13 is the chief Antichrist chapter in the Apocalypse and it closes with a worldwide death threat to all who will not conform to the ruling powers of church and state.

Verses 13 to 19 of the next chapter encourage believers with the assurance that Christ is soon to appear bringing judgment upon the church's enemies. Chapters 15 and 16 tell of the final judgments upon the rebellious world and apostate religion.

The seven last plagues use imagery from Calvary. Their first judgment is a leprous sore on all who have succumbed to false worship. (Christ was treated as a leper suffering "outside the gate" Heb 13:12.) Plagues two and three use blood as their chief symbol (Christ on the cross shed blood from seven wounds). The sun's terrible heat in plague four reminds us of the heat of God's wrath against sin, which our Lord as our Representative endured in our stead. The darkness of the fifth plague is reminiscent of the three hours at Calvary when darkness enshrouded all. These first five plagues are crisply and succinctly set fourth embodying only ten verses. But the last plagues have proportionately a much greater space allotted. We quote in part.

> The sixth angel poured out his bowl on the great river Euphrates, and its water was dried up, to prepare the way for the kings from the East. Then I saw three unclean spirits that looked like frogs; they came out of the mouth of the dragon, out of the mouth of the beast and out of the mouth of the false prophet. They are spirits of demons performing miraculous signs, and they go out to the kings of the whole world, to gather them for the battle on the great day of God Almighty.
>
> "Behold, I come like a thief! Blessed is he who stays awake and keeps his clothes with him, so that he may not go naked and be shamefully exposed."
>
> Then they gathered the kings together to the place that in Hebrew is called Armageddon.
>
> The seventh angel poured out his bowl into the air, and out of the temple came a loud voice from the throne, saying, "It is done!" Then there came flashes of lightning, rumblings, peals of thunder and a severe earthquake. … every island fled away and the mountains could not be found. From the sky huge hailstones of about a hundred pounds each fell upon men.
>
> Rev 16:12-21

The reader should study the whole account from which we have quoted. On Calvary, Christ's personal Armageddon came, when in the thick darkness the spirits of demons tempted him down from the cross. That horror was ended by his triumphant cry, "It is finished!" and the accompanying earthquake, which opened the tombs of many saints and tore the temple veil in two.

But for the present we must attend to the imagery of the sixth plague. Referring to the protagonists of chapter 13, the Revelator has looked back to what precipitated the plagues—the gathering of the world's myriads against the people of God. The sixth plague gives us the result of that murderous onslaught.

Revelation 17:15 tells us that the waters of the Euphrates on which Babylon (Jezebel) sits represent "peoples, multitudes, [and] nations." The word Euphrates itself means "rushing forth," and it is applied in Scripture to invading forces. See Isaiah 8:7,8. Frequently in apocalyptic literature flooding waters signify a persecuting, attacking host. See Daniel 9:26; 11:40 and Revelation 12:15; 13:1.

The "drying up" of the Euphrates symbolizes the destruction of Babylon's attackers. Immediately after the angel's interpretation of the waters supporting the whore we read:

> The beast and the ten horns you saw will hate the
> prostitute. They will bring her to ruin and leave her naked;
> they will eat her flesh and burn her with fire.

> Rev 17:16

We must keep in mind that the whole book of Revelation sets forth the church's experiences in terms parallel to the life and death of its Head. Scholars are agreed "the substance of the Last Things and the substance of the Passion are one and the same" (Austin Farrer). Christ's sacrifice was planned and executed by the union of Satan, apostate Judaism, and the Roman government. (Revelation 16:13 by its reference to the dragon, beast, and false prophet is looking back to that event.) Luke 23:12 says that Pilate and Herod became friends over their attitude to the Messiah. But the union of Judaism and Rome did not last. Forty years after their union in perfidy the Jews rebelled against Rome and suffered the destruction of their Holy City and Temple and the loss of hundreds of thousands of their own people. Revelation 17:16 is drawing from that event which is seen as typical of the break up of the unity between the ultimate Jezebel religion and the existing governments of the world.

How and why shall this take place? Exodus 14:19-20 records how God sent darkness to protect Israel on the verge of what seemed their destruction by that ancient antichrist Pharaoh of Egypt. The same will happen when the world makes its last attempt to wipe out true Christians. But that darkness will be shattered by the appearance of Christ in the eastern heavens as King of kings and Lord of lords accompanied by the angelic hosts.

The manifestation of the Christian's Lord from heaven will vindicate them and fill their enemies with antagonism towards each other especially against their leaders. The multitudes are "dried up" by internecine slaughter.[1] Remember that when the fire of God fell at Carmel the waters surrounding the sacrifice were dried up. The following verses that tell of the typical deliverances of God's people in earlier times illustrate the final Armageddon when "the peoples, multitudes, and tongues" supporting the whore will be "dried up" (Rev 17:15; 16:12).

> When the three hundred trumpets sounded, the Lord caused the men throughout the camp to turn on each other with their swords.
>
> Judg 7:22

---

[1]   Internecine, meaning conflict within a group

Then Saul and his men assembled and went to the battle. They found the Philistines in total confusion, striking each other with their swords.

1 Sam 14:20

As they began to sing and praise, the Lord set ambushes against the men of Ammon and Moab and Mount Seir who were invading Judah, and they were defeated. The men of Ammon and Moab rose up against the men of Mount Seir to destroy and annihilate them. After they finished slaughtering the men from Seir, they helped to destroy one another.

2 Chron 20:22,23

I will summon a sword against Gog on all my mountains, declares the Sovereign Lord. Every man's sword will be against his brother.

Eze 38:21

I will shake the heavens and the earth. I will overthrow royal thrones and shatter the power of the foreign kingdoms. I will overthrow chariots, and their drivers; horses and their riders will fall, each by the sword of his brother.

Hag 2:21,22

How wonderful are the ways of God! Surely he has 10,000 ways of providing for us of which we know nothing.

The remnant of the wicked will be slain by the brightness of Christ's epiphany. See 2 Thessalonians 2:8.

Revelation is a veritable mosaic of OT passages. To understand the Bible's final book, we must study the Old Testament. One of the keys to the sixth plague verses is Isaiah (see 41:2,25; 45:1-3). See also Jeremiah 50:38; 51:13,36,63-64; and Daniel 5. God foretold the coming of Cyrus and his fellow kings of the Medes and Persians against Babylon. They would divert the waters of the great River Euphrates, which ran underneath the city and use the dried up riverbed as a way of access for soldiers into the city. In the antitype Christ will come from the eastern heavens accompanied by his angelic army to overthrow all wickedness and redeem his threatened people.

Darkness in Scripture is often the prelude to great things, and the warning of the resolution of a crisis. Its first use in Genesis 1:2 precedes the light of day and the marvels of subsequent creation. In Genesis 15:12 it is the harbinger of God's covenant with Abraham about his spiritual descendants' inheritance of the earth. See Romans 4:13. In Exodus 14:20 the darkness comes as the beginning of the Red Sea deliverance. A few chapters further on we find God dwelling in darkness at the time of the delivery of the Decalogue. No wonder that Isaiah can write of "the treasures of darkness" (45:3). The fifth plague of Revelation 16 is the sign that the redemption of Christ's people is near. It was even so at Calvary.

The battle of Armageddon is the climax of the age-long controversy between good and evil. Its first shadow was in Eden where Cain slew his brother over the issue of worship. Twenty-four times in Revelation we read concerning worship, for a dominant theme of the book is the challenge to worship the true God who "made the heavens, the earth, the sea and the springs of water" (14:7). The alternative is to "worship the beast and his image and receive his mark" (13:11-18).

The Greek word for worship literally means, "to kiss," and one is reminded of the traitor's kiss in Gethsemane (see also 1 Kings 19:18). Judas is a fitting type of the false prophet—one of the forms of the final

Antichrist who also will pretend to adore the true God while actually betraying him. Seiss has written well on this as he comments on the lamblike beast of Revelation 13.

> Does this beast exercise all the power of the first or kingly beast? In his betrayal of Jesus Judas appears as leader of the band that took Jesus. He acts out the plans of the wicked Jews. They hated Christ, and he sold himself to them. Is the false prophet partly like a lamb, and partly like a dragon? Judas meets Jesus with a kiss and the salutation, "Hail, Master," while he says to His enemies, "Hold Him fast."

He furthers the wish of the rulers of apostate Israel. He counsels them. He leads the way. He accomplishes their end for them. He professed great love for the poor, yet was influenced by thievish avarice. The false prophet presides over the worship of the empire of Antichrist. Judas was ordained an apostle of the Christian faith. Satan enters him, and he is made an apostle of the devil's son. The false prophet serves three-and-a-half years, and that was the length of time Judas was hypocritically in the service of the Saviour. Does the false prophet do great wonders? Judas was gifted with miraculous powers, even though he was a devil, there is no intimation that it has been revoked, and because of this perhaps it was that Satan took possession of him for his own ultimate designs. Jesus sets him at the head of all unbelievers, as Peter was the head of believers, and said of him that he is a demon. Is the false prophet an instigator and patron of idolatry? Judas was blindly and persistently covetous, and "every covetous man is an idolater." He was a suicide, like Ahithtophel and Nero. He "went and hanged himself."

The false prophet instituted a sign or mark for those who follow him; so did Judas. "He gave them a sign" (Matt 26:48). Parts of the 109th Psalm are by inspiration applied to Judas, and the 6th verse must also apply to him: "Set thou a wicked man over him, let Satan stand at his right hand." If he is the false prophet, the man of sin would be his superior, and Satan his great helper. The words as they stand have never been fulfilled; this would fulfil them.

There is something peculiar in the description of what became of Judas after his death. He "went to his own place," as if reserved for some future time and work on the side of evil, as the Two Witnesses … on the side of good. He and the man of sin are the only two to whom the title "Son of perdition" is applied. This is not distinctive of them going into perdition, for that is the common lot of multitudes of others. A son of perdition is rather one begotten and born of perdition, one that comes from hell.

The Apocalypse, p. 335

We do not have to agree with all these comments to see the overall value of the quotation.

We have commented above on the final test over worship, which demands that all make a decision as to whether to accept the mark of the beast or risk death. Appropriately, we now point out that, as with the sixth plague, again we have an allusion to the Old Testament. See Deuteronomy 6:4-9; 11:18; and Ex 13:9,16. The *NASB* uses the word "phylacteries" in its translation of Exodus 13:16. The mark on the hand or the forehead is a counterfeit of God's repeated admonitions to let his laws be the guide of everything human hands do and human minds think. Antichrist has a counterfeit law, as well as a counterfeit gospel, and a counterfeit god.

According to 2 Thessalonians 2:9-12 all who dwell on the earth will be deceived by Satanic deceptions unless they have earlier received the love of the gospel truth. The evidence that we have received God's good news is that we gladly set our wills to do and to think in harmony with his laws. It is characteristic of apocalyptic literature that decisive tests come to professed worshipers, and those tests concern the law of God. See Daniel chapters one, three, and six. In the days of Ahab and Jezebel it was Obadiah, Elijah, and the faithful 7,000 who chose to stand by the sacred Law of God and resist idolatry. They typify the last generation of the people of God who will be threatened by the antitypical Ahab and Jezebel.

The prophetic warnings about the future cannot but distress us. It is helpful to remember that in 18 places in the New Testament "suffering" and "joy" are linked. Christ used the analogy of a woman's birth pangs succeeded by overwhelming joy. As one saint said centuries ago: "All will be well, all will be very well, all manner of things will be well."

CHAPTER FIVE:

GOD'S PROPHYLACTIC AGAINST FALSE WORSHIP AND ALL FORMS OF ANTICHRIST

The worship of Israel under the control of Ahab and Jezebel was a form of nature worship common in their world and constantly reverted to by the professed people of God. The following passages are helpful for our understanding of God's distaste over the folly of his people.

> He did away with the pagan priests appointed by the kings of Judah to burn incense on the high places of the towns of Judah and on those around Jerusalem—those who burned incense to Baal, to the sun and moon, to the constellations and to all the starry hosts. He took the Asherah pole from the temple of the Lord to the Kidron Valley outside Jerusalem and burned it there. He ground it to powder and scattered the dust over the graves of the common people. He also tore down the quarters of the male shrine prostitutes, which were in the temple of the Lord and where women did weaving for Asherah.

> 2 Kings 23:5-7

He then brought me into the inner court of the house of the Lord, and there at the entrance to the temple, between the portico and the altar, were about twenty-five men. With their backs toward the temple of the Lord and their faces toward the east, they were bowing down to the sun in the east.

He said to me, "Have you seen this, son of man? Is it a trivial matter for the house of Judah to do the detestable things they are doing here? Must they also fill the land with violence and continually provoke me to anger? Look at their putting the branch to their nose! Therefore I will deal with them in anger; I will not look on them with pity or spare them. Although they shout in my ears, I will not listen to them."

Eze 8:16-18

The most terrifying warning in the Bible is found in its last pages, and it is a warning against idolatry. While the warning has had relevance in all ages, it finds its fullest fulfilment in the final crisis before the return of Christ. Note the words:

If anyone worships the beast and his image and receives his mark on the forehead or on the hand, he, too, will drink of the wine of God's fury, which has been poured full strength into the cup of his wrath. He will be tormented with burning sulfur in the presence of the holy angels and of the Lamb. And the smoke of their torment rises for ever and ever. There is no rest day or night for those who worship the beast and his image, or for anyone who receives the mark of his name.

Rev 14:9-11

Even when we recall that Scripture says Sodom and Gomorrah were destroyed by everlasting fire, and that the smoke of Edom's destruction would rise for ever and ever, we are not entirely comforted. Semitic hyperbole is present but the warning is none the less real and frightening. It is important to observe that the people who heed this warning are described as obeying God's commandments (Rev 14:12).

We would be wise to remember that God's warnings are often given in order that they might not be fulfilled. God does not wish pain for any of his children, but wilful disobedience always has such fruitage. God wishes us to recognize the evil of sin and to flee from it. Only this can guarantee the safety God wishes for us.

"What God has joined together, let not man put asunder." While originally spoken about marriage, the principle has a wide-ranging significance. We should not study Revelation 14:9-11 without taking into account verses 6-8 of the same passage. Here they are:

> Then I saw another angel flying in midair, and he had the eternal gospel to proclaim to those who live on the earth—to every nation, tribe, language and people. He said in a loud voice, "Fear God and give him glory, because the hour of his judgment has come. Worship him who made the heavens, the earth, the sea and the springs of water."
>
> A second angel followed and said, "Fallen! Fallen is Babylon the Great, which made all the nations drink of the maddening wine of her adulteries."
>
> Rev 14:6-8

From the time Revelation was written this threefold message has had relevance. Idolatry was a great temptation to all in the ancient world towards the end of the first century of the Christian era. Revelation 2:14-23 and other passages make that very clear. The early Christians were subject to pressure from their pagan neighbors to worship the emperor of Rome, and to obey his religious acolytes by offering incense to pagan gods. Such worship was often accompanied by immorality of the worst hue. Remember that Nero had sex with men of all ages and with his own mother.

During the Middle Ages nonconformist Christians were sentenced to the Inquisition and the stake if they refused to practice the Mass and denied homage to the rulers of church and state. Those who read the Scriptures in secret (when available) saw all such worship as idolatry.

Today in the twenty-first century our idolatry is not as crude as in Old Testament times. We have our idols just as surely, but hug them and cherish them and even worship them with a clear conscience. They include wealth, houses and lands, cars, power, prestige, sex, and so on. Ours is a time when secularism rules and is taken for granted by most in the Western world at least. That tide has overswept much of the globe for more than a century. Despite the fact that our brains, electricity, the wind, radiation, and the four great basic realities of the universe (gravity, electro-magnetism, the weak nuclear force, the strong nuclear force) are invisible to us, we instinctively view only the visible as the real. That man or woman, boy or girl who has not surrendered to the currents of culture is viewed as abnormal and even dangerous. The refrain fits most even if not voiced:

"Don't bother me now, don't bother me ever,

I want to be dead for ever and ever."

Think about it. There would never have been an idolater, an atheist, or a secularist had the Law spoken by God's voice and written by his own finger been faithfully observed. In the heart of that Law, and prefaced by the solemn warning "Remember," was God's prophylactic against idolatry. Here it is:

> Remember the Sabbath day by keeping it holy. Six days
> you shall labor and do all your work, but the seventh day
> is a Sabbath to the Lord your God. On it you shall not do
> any work, neither you, nor your son or daughter, nor your
> manservant or maidservant, nor your animals, nor the alien
> within your gates. For in six days the Lord made the heavens
> and the earth, the sea, and all that is in them, but he rested on
> the seventh day. Therefore the Lord blessed the Sabbath day
> and made it holy.

Ex 20:8-11

[We do not here enter upon the vexed question as to whether this law endorses a literal six-day creation. God is described as "resting" and being "refreshed" (Ex 31:17, *KJV*), which is clearly metaphorical language as surely as elements of the inspired account of Genesis contains metaphors. "And God said" (Gen 1:3)—Does God have a larynx? "And God breathed into his nostrils" (2:7)—Does God have lungs? "The Lord God was walking in the garden" (3:8). Is God a biped, or "spirit" as Jesus said (Jn 4:24)? "The Torah speaks in the language of men," taught God's ancient people. The condescension of divine incarnation is apparent from the very first page of the Bible.]

Gnana Robinson, in his Ph.D. dissertation, *The Origin and Development of the Old Testament Sabbath—A Comprehensive Exegetical Approach,* listed a series of texts that conjoin the Sabbath and idolatry and concluded, "These Sabbath-idolatry oppositional references are so many in number that their combination cannot be simply ignored as accidental" (pp. 304-305). The texts referred to are these: Leviticus 19:3,4; 19:29-30; 26:1,2; Ezekiel 20:16, 24; 22:8,9; and 23: 38-39.

The sanctifying of the seventh day of the week is the first religious ordinance mentioned in Scripture. See Genesis 2:1-3. And if the Sabbath was for the first man it was intended also for the last.

At the beginning and end of each dispensation—the patriarchal, the Jewish, and the Christian—the Sabbath is reaffirmed and made a test for the professed people of God. See Genesis 2:1-3; Exodus 16; 20:8-11; Nehemiah 13; Jeremiah 17; Isaiah 56, 58; Matthew 12; Mark 2; Luke 13,14; John 5,9; and Revelation 12:17; 14:6-12. The refrain, "How long do you refuse to keep my commandments and my laws?" in Exodus 16:28 has many echoes throughout Scripture.

The direst warnings and the most wonderful promises are associated with observance of God's prophylactic. In the last verses of Jeremiah 17 Israel was warned that their continued Sabbath profanation would lead to the burning of Jerusalem by fire, whereas the faithful observance of the Sabbath would guarantee the perpetuity of the Holy City. The calamities of 587 B.C. (the prelude to the Babylonian Captivity) and the parallel destruction of Jerusalem in A.D. 70 (the prelude to the worldwide dispersion of the Jews) would never have happened had God's people "remembered." Does not this have tremendous significance for those who in this twenty-first century ignore the fourth commandment? For the promised blessings see Isaiah 56:4-7 and 58:13,14.

Our Saviour died because he willingly bore the sin of the world, but in a purely human sense he died because of his Sabbath reforms. The first time we read of his Jewish opponents conniving to kill him is in Matthew 12:14: "But the Pharisees went out and plotted how they might kill Jesus." See also John 5:6. Our Lord risked his life and mission when he violated Jewish Sabbath traditions and reinstated the meaning of God's primeval ordinance. We find him using more arguments in support of this reform than he ever adduced in any other controversy. Here they are:

From the Edenic account (Mk 2:27,28)

From the Old Testament Sabbath laws (Mt 12:5)

From the story of David recorded in the early prophets (Mt 12:3,4)

From the words of the later prophets (Mt 12:7,8)

From God's continued providential work in nature (Jn 5:17)

From man's everyday experience (Lu 13:15)

From human reason (Mk 3:4; Mt 12:12; and Lu 13:15,16)

From the Messiah's Lordship (Mt 12:6,8)

From conscience (Lu 14:3; Jn 9:13-16, and 37-41).

Thus Christ used sacred history, sacred law, sacred prophecy, divine example, human custom, reason and conscience. We would invite all to find any other institution that Christ laboured so hard to defend and perpetuate. He is as one chiselling away at an inscription partly obscured in order that the writing might stand out clearly. Who cleanses laboriously, and with risk, an old shaky shed, and having cleansed it, burns it down?

Foretelling the downfall of Jerusalem, Christ urged upon his followers the necessity of praying for 40 years that their flight might not need to be in times that would bring pain to body or soul in the winter or on the Sabbath day (Mt 24:20). This was not because the gates of Jerusalem would be shut, because history records that the Jews of the first century, when threatened by invading armies, relaxed Sabbath obligations that they might be unhampered in defending themselves.

Furthermore, Christ's admonition was for all "in Judea," and there were no walls around Judea. After his death, Christ's intimate friends continued to hallow the sacred day. See Luke 23:56.

Let it be carefully observed that while Christ sanctioned Jewish laws apart from the Decalogue, at no time did he expatiate upon them. His teaching as the Saviour of the world was reserved for matters of enduring importance throughout the Christian age. Scholars have long pointed out that the Gospel writers only included in their accounts of Christ's life those matters pertinent for the church of their day.

Is it sheer coincidence that our Lord completed his saving work on the sixth day on the eve of the Sabbath, once more proclaiming, "It is finished" and entered into Sabbath rest? Is it sheer coincidence that the Last Adam again on the sixth day has his side opened, and falls into a deep sleep that he might procure to himself a bride—as Adam in Eden? Does not all this signify that the new era has dawned with the Cross, and that it provides the substance prefigured in the old era? So the crucified Christ keeps the Sabbath in death, as well as in life, just as he had at the time of his creation of the world. Henceforth the Sabbath would teach that because of Christ's finished work, all who believe enter into continual rest of heart, despite their infirmities (Heb 4:3).

Our Lord performed many miracles on the holy day and of these, seven are recorded—seven which are amazing in their scope. These miracles include blessings brought to those of varying age and sex and condition, and from each dominant sector of human life—the sacred (in church), the domestic (at home) and in public (along the way). Note the following:

Healing the demoniac in the synagogue (Mk 1:21-28)

Healing of Simon's mother-in-law at home (Mk 1:29-31)

Healing in the synagogue of man with withered hand (Mk 3:1-6)

Healing of bent-over woman in the synagogue (Lu 13:10-17)

Healing of man with dropsy at home (Lu 14:1-6)

Healing of impotent man at Bethesda (Jn 5:1-20)

Healing of blind man on the road (Jn 9:1-41)

The range in people, places, and needs is impressive. A young man (the beggar of John 9), an old man who has been almost 40 years paralysed, an old woman (Peter's mother-in-law), and the woman bent over for 18 years—and others who were probably in middle life—all find blessing beyond compare on the holy day. This blessing is not only bestowed in the holy place of church but in the domestic center of daily life, as well as on the busy highway of social and business intercourse.

It is not my concern here to enter into the controversy over the seventh versus the first day of the week as the Christian Sabbath. Years ago I wrote a comprehensive volume on this topic, *The Forgotten Day*, and my views remain the same. But we are here concerned with the fourth commandment as such. Until the Industrial Revolution reached its height almost all in the Western world who were Christian believed in the binding obligation of that commandment in the heart of the Decalogue prefaced by "Remember." Whether one reads biography, theology, or commentaries the story is the same till about the twentieth century. But even here we find the greatest theologian of that day extolling the Sabbath commandment in ways that almost verge on hyperbole. Listen to Karl Barth:

This is the most detailed of all the Ten Commandments.
Again with the second, it outwardly characterised most

clearly the attitude of Old Testament man, his obedience or disobedience. Understood in its new—or rather its true—form, in its first and final meaning, it was surprisingly quickly and self-evidently seen to be valid and authoritative in New Testament Christianity as a rule which must naturally apply forthwith to the old, the new, the one people of God.

In general, theological ethics has handled this command of God, or the one command of God in this particular application, with a casualness and feebleness that certainly do not match its importance in Holy Scripture or its decisive material significance.

What does the Sabbath commandment say? It speaks of a limiting of man's activity to the extent that is, generally speaking, his own work, his own undertaking and achievement, the job he does for his livelihood and in the service of the community. It says that, in deference to God and to the heart and meaning of His work, there must be from time to time an interruption, a rest, a deliberate non-continuation, a temporal pause, to reflect on God and His work and to participate consciously in the salvation provided by Him and to be awaited from Him. It says that man's own work is to be performed as a work bounded by this continually recurring interruption. This interruption is the holy day.

The Sabbath commandment explains all the other commandments, or all the other forms of the one commandment. It is thus to be placed at their head. By demanding man's abstention and resting from his own works, it explains that the commanding God, who has created man and enabled and commissioned him to do his own work, is the

God who is gracious to man in Jesus Christ. Thus it points him away from everything that he himself can will and achieve and back to what God is for him and will do for him. It reminds man of God's plan for him, of the fact that He has already carried it out, and that in His revelation He will execute both His will with him and his work for and toward him. It points him to the Yes which the Creator has spoken to him, his creature, and which he has continually and at last definitely acknowledged, which He has made true and proved true once and for all in Jesus Christ. It summons him to hold to this Yes and not to anything else. And that is why it commands him to keep holy the Sabbath day.

If we link the significance of the holy day in salvation history and its eschatological significance, and if we remember that in both instances we are concerned with its relationship to the particularity of God's omnipotent grace, we shall understand at once, and not without a certain awe, the radical importance, the almost monstrous range of the Sabbath commandment. By the distinction of this day, by the summons to celebrate it according to its meaning, this command sets man and the human race in terribly concrete confrontation with their Creator and Lord, with His particular will and Word and work, and with the goal, determined and set by Him, of the being of all His creatures, which means also the inexorable end of the form of their present existence. This commandment is total. It discovers and claims man in his depths and from his utmost bounds.

Thus the Sabbath commandment in its particularity explains all the other forms of the one divine commandment.

In relation to the One who commands, it explains what is always and in all cases commanded. It does not explain this abstractly but concretely, by indicating the seventh day and the succession of sevenths (and therefore no less than the seventh part of the time granted to man) as the special time of the gracious God which it expects man to keep free for the gracious God. The concern of this particular day is indirectly that of all the other days as well. This particular thing is the meaning of all the divine commands.

The Sabbath commandment requires of man that he understand and live his life on this basis. It thus demands of him that he believe in God as his Ruler and Judge, and that he let his self-understanding in every conceivable form be radically transcended, limited and relativised by this faith, or rather by the God in whom he believes. It demands that he know himself only in his faith in God, that he will and work and express himself only in this imposed and not selected renunciation, and that on the basis of this renunciation he actually dare in it all to be a new creature, a new man. This is the astonishing requirement of the Sabbath commandment.

De Quervain is only too right in this respect. "Where the holy day becomes the day of man, society and humanity wither away and the demons rule." …

The holy day is a sign, and keeping it holy an exercise, of man's freedom before God and of the special responsibility towards Him in which he is man, the human creature. As the regular observance of a definite portion of time, keeping the holy day is the most visible and, because of this day's special meaning, the most comprehensive form of this special responsibility.

"The Work of Creation," Chapter IX, *Church Dogmatics,* Vol, 3, part 1, pp. 3-366, (but see especially pp. 41-73)

Consider the extravagant terms Barth uses in connexion with the fourth commandment. He speaks of its "decisive material significance," its "radical importance," "the almost monstrous range," of it, etc.

And thereby he only echoes what the best and most spiritual of Christians have usually said down through the ages. See for example Bishop Ryle, Bishop Wordsworth, Dr Patrick Fairbairn, Spurgeon, Maclaren, and a host of others.

It is difficult to fault Dr Robert Dabney when he affirms: "If the great duty of worship is essentially and morally binding, this necessary provision for compliance (the Sabbath) is also essentially and morally binding." This is spelled out in detail in Dabney's *Lectures in Systematic Theology,* pp. 376-397.

And there the case for the perpetuity of the fourth commandment might be rested, for no Christian denies the priority of worship. Has God made no provision for it?

In our day nothing is more striking when we consider the behaviour of millions of professing believers than their failure to take the fourth commandment seriously. Not one in a hundred does. They surrender an hour for church attendance and then spend the rest of the day according to their own preferences. But consider what Scripture requires for true observance of the fourth commandment:

If you keep your feet from breaking the Sabbath and from doing as you please on my holy day, if you call the Sabbath a delight and the Lord's holy day honorable, and if you honor it by not going your own way and not doing as you please or speaking idle words, then you will find your joy in the Lord and I will cause you to ride on the heights of the land and to feast on the inheritance of your father Jacob.

Isa 58:13,14

Would not Isaiah be scandalized by the universal careless behavior of today's Christians? And would not Jeremiah anticipate soon coming judgment on those who expect to get eternity, but who refuse God even one day per week?

We have substituted our own idols for God—such as wealth, sex, pleasure, money, ease, power, prestige—and ignored the one heaven-sent luxury which could save us from such folly. Where are those of the twice-born church, who will protest against this idolatry as vigorously as Elijah did in his day?

CHAPTER 6:

THE EXCUSE FOR ATTEMPTED GENOCIDE

"Art thou he that troubleth Israel?" (1 Kings 18:17, *KJV*)

Guilty men rationalize to justify their wicked deeds. Pharaoh saw in the phenomenal growth of Israel's numbers a threat to Egypt and determined to deal with them as all tyrants have always done—bloody force. Another leader, this time the head of a professed people of God, Caiaphas, satirically declared, "It is better that one man die and the whole nation perish not" (Jn 11). The "one man" of course was Christ, and the nation was that of Israel. Caiaphas determined that it was better to surrender Christ to the cruelty of Roman law than to have Jewry in any way threatened.

Thirty years later Rome burned and suspicion fastened on Nero. To remove the growing antagonism the emperor needs must find a scapegoat. He chose the Christians. Says Frederick W. Farrar in his *The Early Days of Christianity*, p. 34ff:

> It is clear that a shedding of blood—in fact, some form
> or other of human sacrifice—was imperatively demanded by
> popular feeling as an expiation of the ruinous crime that had

plunged so many thousands into the depths of misery. In vain had the Sibylline Books been once more consulted, and in vain had public prayer been offered, in accordance with their directions, to Vulcan and the goddesses of Earth and Hades. In vain had the Roman matrons walked in procession in dark robes, and with their long hair unbound, to propitiate the insulted majesty of Juno, and to sprinkle with seawater her ancient statue. In vain had largesse been lavished upon the people, and propitiatory sacrifices offered to the gods. In vain had public banquets been celebrated in honour of various deities.

A crime had been committed, and Romans had perished unavenged. Blood cried for blood, before the sullen suspicion against Nero could be averted, or the indignation of heaven appeased. Nero had always hated, persecuted, and exiled the philosophers, and no doubt, so far as he knew anything of the Christians—so far as he saw among his own countless slaves any who had embraced this superstition, which the elite of Rome described as not only new, but "execrable" and "malefic"—he would hate their gravity and purity, and feel for them that raging envy which is the tribute that virtue receives from vice. Moreover, St. Paul, in all probability, had recently stood before his tribunal; and although he had been acquitted on the special charges of turbulence and profanation, respecting which he had appealed to Caesar, yet during the judicial enquiry Nero could hardly have failed to hear from the emissaries of the Sanhedrin many fierce slanders of a sect which was everywhere spoken against.

When once the Christians were pointed out to the popular vengeance, many reasons would be adduced to prove their connexion with the conflagration. The Temple had perished—and were they not notorious enemies of the temples? Did not popular rumour charge them with nocturnal orgies? ... Suspicions of incendiarism were sometimes brought against the Jews; but the Jews were not in the habit of talking, as these sectaries were, about a fire that would consume the world—rejoicing in the prospect of that fiery consummation. Nay, more, when Pagans had bewailed the destruction of the city and the loss of the ancient monuments of Rome, had not these pernicious people used ambiguous language, as though they joyously recognised in these events the signs of a coming end?

Even when they tried to suppress all outward tokens of exultation, had they not listened to the fears and lamentations of their fellow-citizens with some sparkle in the eyes, and had they not answered with something of triumph in their tones? There was a satanic plausibility, which dictated the selection of these particular victims. Because they hated the wickedness of the world, with its ruthless games and hideous idolatries, they were accused of hatred of the whole human race. This was sufficient to ruin a body of men who scorned the sacrifices of heathendom, and turned away with abhorrence from its banquets and gaieties. The cultivated classes looked down upon Christians with a disdain that would hardly even mention them without an apology, The *canaille* of Pagan cities insulted them with obscene inscription and blasphemous pictures on the very walls of the places where they met. Nay, they were popularly known by nickname. ... untranslatable terms of opprobrium derived from the fagots with which they were burned and the stakes to which they were chained. Even the heroic courage, which they displayed, was described as being sheer obstinacy and stupid fanaticism.

But in the method chosen for the punishment of these saintly innocents Nero gave one more proof of the close connexion between effeminate aestheticism and sanguinary callousness. … History has given many proofs that no man is more systematically heartless than a corrupted debauchee. Like people, like prince. In the then condition of Rome Nero well knew that a nation "cruel, by their sports to blood inured" would be most likely to forget their miseries, and condone their suspicions by mixing games and gaiety with spectacles of refined and atrocious cruelty, of which for eighteen centuries, the most passing record has sufficed to make men's blood run cold.

Tacitus tells us that, "those who confessed were first seized, and then on their evidence *a huge multitude* were convicted, not so much on the charge of incendarianism as for their hatred of mankind. Compressed and obscure as the sentence is, Tacitus clearly means to imply by the "confession" to which he alludes the confession of Christianity; and though he is not sufficiently generous to acquit the Christians absolutely of all complicity in the great crime, he distinctly says that they were made the scapegoats of a general indignation. The phrase "a huge multitude"—is one of the few existing indications of the number of martyrs in the first persecution, and of the number of Christians in the Roman Church. When the historian says that they were convicted on the charge of "hatred against mankind" he shows how completely he confounds them with the Jews, against whom he elsewhere brings the accusation of "hostile feelings towards all except themselves."

Then the historian adds one casual but frightful sentence—a sentence, which flings a dreadful light on the cruelty of Nero and the Roman mob. He adds:

And various forms of mockery were added to enhance their dying agonies. Covered with the skins of wild beasts, they were doomed to die by the mangling of dogs, or by being nailed to crosses; or to be set on fire and burnt after twilight by way of nightly illumination. Nero offered his own gardens for this show, and gave a chariot race, mingling with the mob in the dress of a charioteer, or actually driving about among them. Hence, guilty as the victims were, and deserving of the worst punishments, a feeling of compassion towards them began to arise, as men felt that they were being immolated not for any advantage to the commonwealth, but to glut the savagery of a single man.

Imagine that awful scene, once witnessed by the silent obelisk in the square before St. Peter's at Rome! Imagine it, that we may realise how vast is the change which Christianity has wrought in the feelings of mankind! There, where the vast dome now rises, were once the gardens of Nero. They were thronged with gay crowds, among whom the Emperor moved in his frivolous degradation—and on every side were men dying on their cross of shame. Along the paths of those gardens on the autumn nights were ghastly torches, blackening the ground beneath them with streams of sulphurous pitch, and each of these living torches was a martyr in his shirt of fire. And in the amphitheatre hard by, in sight of twenty thousand spectators, famished dogs were tearing to pieces some of the best and purest of men and women, hideously disguised in the skins of bears or wolves. Thus did Nero baptise in the blood of martyrs the city, which was to be for ages the capital of the world!

These comments by Farrar are worthy of close study. See how evil is the heart of man. See what he is capable of! Consider the necessity for a resurrection of the wicked at the end of time that they might be judged for their evil deeds! And marvel at the love and faith of the early Christians who were faithful unto death, and what a death! We shall see them again, singing songs of triumph!

But in one place Farrar is wrong. He assumes in that last paragraph that feelings of modern men would prevent any such thing happening again. But Farrar lived before the Holocaust. And perhaps he had not yet given full attention to the biblical scenario of the end of the world and the coming time of great tribulation. We have no excuse for such naivety. Think also on the fact that from Calvary onwards Christians believed in a final cleansing of the whole earth by fire. The fire that fell on the Carmel sacrifice in the days of Elijah was not only an endorsement of true religion then. It was a warning of devastating fire as the end for all who pursue idolatrous lives rather than worship the Creator. See 2 Kings 1:10-12 and Revelation 11:5. The brightness of the returning King of kings will dry up the remnant of the "multitudes, peoples, and tongues" symbolized by the River Euphrates supporting the antitypical Jezebel as surely as the divine fire dried up the waters in Elijah's trenches.

In the centuries that followed, fiendish crime followed fiendish crime, but the most terrible of all was the Massacre of St Bartholomew. Beginning in Paris, but extending to the provinces, neither age nor sex were spared. Old and young, revered ancient, or the tiny sucking child had to die. The butchery continued for two months. Seventy thousand Protestants, the very flower of the nation, were murdered. (That number is disputed. Most modern accounts make it far less, but none the less an unforgettable and inexcusable massacre.) The Pope, Innocent III, decreed that the *Te Deum* be sung in Rome, and there was great rejoicing in Madrid. But the rest of the world, both Catholic and Protestant, was horrified by the massacre.

That was in the year 1572. Years later came the French Revolution when both justified and unjustified anger issued in life-destroying violence. This event will be discussed later in this volume.

Most well known of all such barbarisms was the Holocaust of our own time when between five and six million Jews were made scapegoats for all Europe's problems by the racist Adolf Hitler. Again old and young, the aged and the babes, female as well as male perished because they were regarded as the troublers of the world.

And what shall we say of September 11, 2001? Has not the extreme edge of militant Islam always blamed Western democracies for their humiliations? So hundreds die terribly because of the twisted thinking of fanatics. But again there were rationalizations. Was not the West the troubler of Islam?

The chief fulfilment of this scenario lies yet ahead. The world is shrinking because of technology and communication, and the shrinking brings much pain. The rich become richer and the poor become poorer. Governments are terrified by the nuclear threat. Nine million shipping containers enter U.S. ports every year, and only five percent are examined. Some of the multiple nuclear materials from the former USSR are now undoubtedly in America, and in the hands of Al Quaeda representatives. It takes little trouble now to assemble a nuclear weapon. Even refined uranium is not needed, only radioactive materials that exist in abundance—not only in hospitals, but also at many other sites.

A "dirty" bomb is simple in composition. An ordinary bomb is used with it to trigger a nuclear explosion. Suppose a dozen of these were planted in the largest cities of America? Suppose one was exploded in New York or Washington? What then? Then the U.S. Government would be told that unless they surrendered to the demands of militant Islam another 11 cities would be destroyed. And, as goes America, so goes the world. The world could become Islam's almost overnight. And this despite the fact that most people of Muslim faith seek only a quiet life and have no desire to see cruelty wreaked outside their borders.

The day is coming when economic, racial, terrorist, financial and disease threats will be overwhelming. It will have been demonstrated that education, science, technology and politics have all failed to ameliorate human woes. The masses will demand scapegoats and they will be found. Nonconformists will be hated, and of these nonconformists Christians stand preeminent. Have they not protested against war, greed, dishonesty in politics, racial hatred, and oppression of the poor by the rich? Christians will be declared to be the troublers of the world. And, ultimately, it will be decided by governments and apostate religious advisers that, for the sake of the world's safety, the nonconformists must be eliminated.

But what will be the real source of the world's ever increasing pains? Elijah tells us the answer. To the idolatrous king, spouse of the sunworshipper Jezebel, he declared, "You are the real troubler of Israel because you have forsaken the commandments of God" (see 1 Kings 18:18).

How simple and obvious is the real solution to the world's problems! "When all else fails, follow the directions." God has given us directions for our wellbeing. They are simple, so that even children can understand them. No PhDs are needed. Just read the Ten Commandments, the Sermon on the Mount, and 1 Corinthians chapter 13. There is more than enough there to heal the world's woes. But men reject these divine directions. They must have their own way—a way of greed and lust. And because the eye cannot see itself, so the wicked of the Last Days will not even consider that they are to blame for earth's woes. They will find scapegoats—the Elijahs of the end-time. Be prepared, and live now by exultant faith in preparation for that testing time!

CHAPTER SEVEN:
THE RESTORING OF THE ALTAR

Our Lord after his Transfiguration told his most trusted disciples, Peter, James, and John, the truth about the prophecy of Malachi 4. "To be sure, Elijah comes and will restore all things. But I tell you, Elijah has already come, and they did not recognize him. ..." Then the disciples understood that he was talking to them about John the Baptist" (Mt 17:11-13).

The most obvious meaning of our Lord's words is that Malachi's prophecy yet had a future fulfilment, although John the Baptist was the immediate and primary one. "Elijah will restore all things." This seems to be an allusion not only to Malachi 4 but to 1 Kings 18:30 where we read concerning Elijah that, "he repaired the altar of the Lord which was in ruins." Revelation 11:1 may help us also. The prophet is there told to measure the Temple of God and the altar, as well as the worshipers.

What could this mean? The altar, the place of sacrifice, prominent both in the Mosaic tabernacle and Solomon's temple is central for worship. It reminds everybody that God in the person of his Son would shed his blood for the guilty race that pardon might be given to all repentant souls. There was another altar, not for sacrifice, but associated with believing prayers sanctified by the incense of the righteousness of Christ. It was central in the first apartment, the holy place, before the inner veil.

In 1 Kings 18 the altar of sacrifice is clearly intended, because there Elijah's offering was consumed by fire. What is meant by a latter-day restoring and repairing? It is clear from Luke 18:8 and Matthew 24:28 that our Lord knew that society before his return, including much professed religion, would be like a rotting carcass and that true faith would be a rare thing in the earth. But a work is to be done for the faithful by Christ's witnesses in the Last Days. First and foremost, the everlasting gospel, the objective historical gospel of the New Testament, is to be clarified and exalted—"the good, glad, and merry tidings, which makes the heart to sing and the feet to dance" (Tyndale). This exalting of the gospel will include the gospel's finale—eschatology— the Last Things that will vindicate and implement all signified by Calvary. Second, there is to be a call out of Babylon, that is, a warning against a predominant, Jezebel-like, religion (see Revelation 18:1-4). Similarly, they will be warned against the idolatrous worship imposed by law through the "beast" and the "false prophet." Third, they will be challenged to be faithful to "the commandments of God and the testimony of Jesus" (Rev 12:17). This will involve genuine worship of the Creator of heaven and earth in harmony with his precepts. Revelation 14:12 tells the same story.

In this regard it is important to recognize that John the Revelator never uses the word "law" (*nomos*) in his Apocalypse. There had been so much controversy in the first decades of the church over law (as witnessed by Paul's Epistles), that John uses now three other terms for that part of the Mosaic Law that was of permanent significance—the Decalogue.

From the Apostle Paul's day to our own there has been much "striving about the law," which has frequently proved "unprofitable and vain." With good reason did Martin Luther declare that one of the most important tests of true theology is the ability "rightly to deal law and gospel."

It is the worst type of religion when salvation is made to hinge on the punctilious observance of law as the way of being right with God. This is legalism and is rejected from Matthew to Revelation. On the other hand it is an awfully bad sign to be out of love with the Law of God, for all Bible saints and their successors have esteemed it as a sacred reflection of the character and will of the Creator.

The Scylla and Charybdis menacing every mind not illuminated by the Holy Spirit are legalism and antinomianism. While the former by law, "would frustrate the grace of God," the latter would, "make void the law through faith." The Pharisees of Christ's day and the Zwickau prophets of the Reformation era typify the extreme forms of these perversions. Remarkable indeed is the fact that the great symbols of the Protestant faith at the time of the Reformation successfully steered between these doctrinal monsters and affirmed the perpetuity of the moral requirements of God once written with the divine finger on tables of stone.

Since the nineteenth century there has been an increasing departure in Protestant circles from the landmarks of the Reformation, and we would anticipate that this would be true with reference to the biblical code of duty, as well as in other areas of Scripture. It appears that the battle against antinomianism needs to be fought again and this time more conclusively than in the sixteenth century.

The whole New Testament condemns Law as a method of salvation but upholds it as a standard of righteousness. And in the last pages of Holy Writ the sacredness of the Decalogue, as interpreted by the apostles, is upheld. Central to all the visions of the Apocalypse is the heavenly sanctuary. See Revelation 1:12; 4:1; 8:3; and 15:5, etc. In 15:5 John refers to this sanctuary as "the tabernacle of the testimony," thus directing us in the *omega* of Scripture to the use of this same term found in the *alpha* of the inspired Word. In the Pentateuch, "the tabernacle of the testimony," is referred to repeatedly. Why was it given this name? Because in its heart resided the ark which housed the "tables of the testimony"—the Ten Commandments. The term "testimony" as found in the Bible's first five books means the Ten Commandment and only them. The recurrence of the term in the last book of Scripture identifies these same commandments as still central in the plan of God during the Christian dispensation and obedience to them an integral part of true worship. Wherever in Scripture "testimony" is linked to the "tabernacle," the Decalogue and the Decalogue alone is in focus. Revelation 15:5 assures us that the sacred will of God is the cynosure of all heavenly beings and the very basis of divine acts. On earth it was covered by the golden mercy seat, which received the sprinkling of the atoning blood of sacrifice. Law and mercy must ever go together.

Two other terms are used in Revelation for the Ten. They are "covenant" and "commandments." A passage similar to 15:5 is 11:19 where we read of the "ark of his testament." "Testament" is the same term in the Greek original as "covenant." Between these two key texts are others which describe the people of God as, "keeping the commandments of God" (12:17; 14:12). Other Bible summaries, such as Galatians 5:6; 6:15; and 1 Corinthians 7:19, show that those who are new creatures in Christ by faith observe the commandments of God—those commandments, which in contrast to circumcision and other ceremonial observances, endure for all ages.

Let it not be thought for one moment that this biblical emphasis on law is a rigorous, painful demand for sinners. That law tells us the primary things we need to know to be happy and successful in our Christian walk. First, it tells us that the universe is not the product of chance, but is run by law. It is a universe, not a multiverse. Second, it warns us to put first things first (thus the early commandments have to do with our relationship to our Maker). Third, it assures us that people are more important than things. "Things" are emphasized only in the last commandment.

"Repairing" of the altar of God in these Last Days will include the setting forth of the true relationship between law and gospel, and it will warn against prevailing perversions of both. Yet there is more.

How many millions have become atheists through the presentation of the pagan teachings of limbo, purgatory, and eternal hell-fire? True, the Bible does speak of "everlasting fire," but the context shows that this signifies fire that is everlasting in its effects, not in its process. See Jude 7; and 2 Peter 2:6. The Bible refers to soul and spirit about 1,700 times, but not once are we told that either can survive without a body. The fate of the wicked is to "perish," according to the most well known text of the Bible.

When God's glorious truths are clearly presented in the Last Days, it will be emphasized that there is eternal life in Christ and in Christ alone (1 Jn 5:11,12), and that only he or she who has committed themselves to the Saviour of Calvary with all their hearts, minds, and strength has eternal life. So, through eternity, all living beings will joyfully praise God, Revelation 5:13.

Inevitably involved in the true presentation of the gospel is the concept of stewardship. We are not our own. We have been bought with a price. All we have is the purchase of the blood of Christ and is to be used to his glory. This involves prayerful careful management of all God has lent us—material goods, health, time, the gospel, and opportunities to do good. It will be made plain that the believer's body is a temple not a tavern, and the final evidence of the indwelling Spirit "temperance" (Gal 5:23) must be extolled. See 1 Corinthians 9:24-27; 2 Corinthians 6:16; 1 Corinthians 6:19-20; and Romans 12:1.

Under the guidance of the Spirit all God's good gifts will be used to his glory including music and every human talent. Singing in worship, for example, will not degenerate to purely subjective emphasis on human feelings and experience, but it will, as in the days of the Wesleys, exalt what God has done on Calvary for his rebel children.

Chapter Eight:
The God Who Answers by Fire—
He is God

Fire in Scripture is frequently a symbol of the powerful, enlivening, purging Holy Spirit (Mt 3:11; Acts 2:3). And remember, "if anyone does not have the Spirit of Christ, he does not belong to Christ" (Rom 8:9).

Without doubt all the gifts of the Spirit, including miraculous powers, will be manifest in the closing proclamation of the gospel. But always more important than the gifts (all of which can be counterfeited) is the fruit of the Spirit—that fruit described in Galatians 5 and which, in full blossom, can never be counterfeited.

1 Kings 18 and Revelation chapters 11 and 13 emphasize the role of the third Member of the Godhead in the final crisis. Antichrist will work miracles purporting to be the miraculous work of God's Spirit, but like the magicians of Egypt his power will be limited. Only those indwelt by Christ will be empowered over men and demons and proclaim the Word to every nation, kindred, tongue and people. They, like Elijah, will work miracles authenticating their message.

To understand the coming Pentecost that will empower the church of the twice born (not a denomination) to give the gospel to the world, one needs to study closely the book of Acts. That book should be called, "The Acts of the Risen Christ through His Spirit," for chapter after chapter speaks of the Spirit and his work. Acts chapter 2 was what many Christians call "the early rain," but the "latter rain" (Elijah's rain, 1 Kings 18:45) will make possible the complete fulfilment of Revelation 18:1-4; 10:1-7; and 14:6-12.

Ours is a post-Christian world. Yet Christ predicted that in the last generation, "this gospel of the kingdom will be preached in the whole world as a testimony to all nations, and then the end will come." How can this be? How can the weakness of the present Christian church become strength, its whisper a clarion call? How can the apathy of unbelievers be stirred into conscious, clamouring need? One entire book of Scripture is devoted to the answer. In Acts lies the dynamite, which will yet blast the doddering inefficiency of the church and shake the spiritual nonchalance of the world.

The book begins with a promise and a program. "You will receive power when the Holy Spirit comes on you, and you will be my witnesses in Jerusalem, and in all Judea and Samaria, and to the ends of the earth" (Acts 1:8).

This verse not only comprehends a table of contents for the book of Acts—which opens with the gospel being proclaimed at Jerusalem and closes with its announcement in Rome—it is also the evangelistic charter for the Christian church. The book itself is the church's missionary manual. The Book of Acts is the only unfinished book of Scripture. Read the last verses and note how they leave the reader dangling in the air.

Why? Because the task discussed in its pages is not yet completed. The real conclusion to Acts will be written in letters of fire, the fire of the Holy Spirit igniting again the gospel flame he lit at Pentecost.

John's Gospel, which immediately precedes Acts, closed with the story of the Apostles unprofitably fishing all night. In the morning, Christ, standing on the shore half hidden by mists, turned their failure into unprecedented success. The empty net was suddenly filled to the breaking point.

This glorious event is a fitting introduction to Acts. Henceforth, Christ would no longer be visible in the fishing vessel of the church. He would stand on heaven's shore. His voice would be conveyed by the wind of the Spirit.

Yet as his followers obeyed his instructions, success would surely come. The gospel commission would be fulfilled, and the gospel net filled to overflowing.

The introduction to Luke's earlier book, the Gospel, had spoken of "all that Jesus began to do and to teach" (Acts 1:1). Now in the Book of Acts the chronicle is continued, and we are told of all Jesus continued to do by the operation of his Spirit in the first believers.

Luke's book shows that it was the Spirit of Christ, who directed the acts of the early leaders of the church. The book, therefore, prepares us to acknowledge the guidance of that same Spirit in the teachings of those leaders found in the Epistles that follow Acts.

A famous Greek play by Aeschylus gives a magnificent description of the fire signals by which the hero made known to his queen the capture of distant Troy. The victory flame flashed from mountaintop to mountaintop, leaping over the seas and plain till its radiance lighted the city of Argos. Even so does Acts portray the beacon lights of Christianity flashing from Jerusalem to Antioch, from Antioch to Ephesus to Troas to Philippi—from thence to Athens and Corinth until finally the holy flame was kindled in the very palace of the Caesars.

The light of the world had dawned in a tiny Judean village and brightened the hills of Galilee. Then apparently it had been eclipsed at Calvary. Now, the Book of Acts shows that it had not gone out at all, as its friends had feared. Instead it flickers and flares and flashes till its brilliance gleams across the Aegean, and fills Asia and Greece and Italy with such a light as had never before shone on land or sea.

Both the message and the method by which the early church "turned the world upside down" in a single generation is presented clearly by this book. Both comprise the pattern which, when copied, will enable the church to complete its Elijah task, and help put an end to the scandal of sin, sorrow, and death.

The message is repeatedly said to be the gospel of Jesus Christ. Not psychology, not politics, not ethics, not good advice, but the good news that God conquered sin through the ministry, death, and resurrection of his Son. This is the theme that set the world alight. The apostles "never stopped teaching and proclaiming the good news that Jesus is the Christ" (5:42).

But what was this preaching of Christ? Did the apostles proclaim merely the demands of the Sermon on the Mount? Did they present only Christ's holy character and matchless life?

If this had been the case, then Christ himself—in the days of his Judean ministry—should have gathered his followers by the thousands. His later preachers would have gathered only hundreds, inasmuch as the reality would have been more powerful than the mere record.

But the opposite is true. It was the disciples who won thousands, not Jesus. Why? Because the Apostles preached the significance of Christ's life, death, and resurrection in a way that had not been possible before Calvary. They told of the forgiveness of sins, of the resurrection of the body, and of life everlasting, all made possible by the atoning death of God's Son.

Listen to their words, which when proclaimed afresh, will recover for the church her ancient power. They will repair God's neglected altar of worship.

> "God exalted him. ... as Prince and Savior that he might give repentance and forgiveness of sins ..." (Acts 5:31).

> "Repent and be baptized, every one of you, in the name of Jesus Christ for the forgiveness of your sins. And you will receive the gift of the Holy Spirit" (2:38).

> "Repent, then, and turn to God, so that your sins may be wiped out ..." (3:19).

> "Therefore, my brothers, I want you to know that through Jesus the forgiveness of sins is proclaimed to you. Through him everyone who believes is justified from everything you could not be justified from by the Law of Moses" (13:38,39).

> "All the prophets testify about him that everyone who believes in him receives forgiveness of sins through his name" (10:43).

The Apostles saw that, objectively, Christ is all; and that, subjectively, faith is all. Salvation and acceptance with God is not something we attain, but something we *obtain*. Salvation is a gift to be received because of the infinite sacrifice of God on our behalf.

"One died for all, and therefore all died" (2 Cor 5:14). Because Christ represented all people as the Last Adam, his death is counted as our death; his resurrection is counted as our resurrection. We are free from guilt and condemnation in him. We are "complete in him," "accepted in the beloved," because, "when we were yet God's enemies, we were reconciled to him through the death of his Son" (Col 2:10, KJV; Eph 1:6, KJV; and Rom 5:10).

Therefore Paul wrote that it is our privilege to be:

> Strengthened with all power, according to his glorious might so that you may have great endurance and patience, and joyfully giving thanks to the Father, who has qualified you to share in the inheritance of the saints in the kingdom of light. For he has rescued us from the dominion of darkness and brought us into the kingdom of the Son he loves, in whom we have redemption, the forgiveness of sins.
>
> Col 1: 11-14

This was the message of the conquering church in apostolic times. God has delivered humanity. Sin has been atoned for. Our acceptance of so great salvation by the empty hand of faith brings a perfect standing with heaven, and a new heart and life.

What about the method by which the church spread the good news? The answer is given 71 times in this book, for that is the number of times the Holy Spirit is mentioned.

The Book of Acts is the record of the Spirit who could not be given fully to the church till Christ was glorified (see John 7:37-39). What someone has called, "the irresistible might of weakness," is possible only though the ministry of God's Spirit. "'Not by might, not by power, but by my Spirit', says the Lord Almighty" (Zech 4:6).

This ascension gift of Christ, this promise of the Father, this power of the resurrection, is the secret of the progress of the Christian church.

As Dr Scroggie has written:

> Thus "the key is hanging on the door" when we read at
> the very commencement of Acts the significant expression
> 'through the Holy Spirit' (1:2). All so-called Christian work,
> which is not "through the Holy Spirit", falls barren and lifeless
> to the ground.

How did believers in the first century receive the Holy Spirit? What did they have to do?

The second question reminds us of the natural error of the sinful heart, thinking that the gift of God can be bought (see Acts 8:20). The Gospels warn us against this dead-end route: "Then they asked him, 'What must we do to do the works God requires?' Jesus answered: 'The work of God is this: to believe in the one he has sent'" (Jn 6:28,29).

The teaching of Acts echoes Jesus' teaching in the Gospels. After Peter had preached Christ in the power of the Spirit on the Day of Pentecost, multitudes were convinced and cried out, "What shall we do?" (Acts 2:37). This is the same emphasis on human works, which tragically reverberates throughout Scripture, even since Adam and Eve sought to hide their nakedness by their own tailoring.

Peter's counsel rebukes the human tendency to earn righteousness:

> Peter replied, "Repent and be baptized every one of you,
> in the name of Jesus Christ for the forgiveness of your sins.
> And you will receive the gift of the Holy Spirit. The promise

is for you and your children and for all who are far off—for all whom the Lord our God will call."

Acts 2:38,39

Only perfect obedience to God's immutable law could earn the priceless treasure of the indwelling God, but such obedience is possible only to one in whom God already dwells. Thus Adam and Eve, made to be temples of the Holy Spirit, could fulfil the law so long as they looked to God.

But it is not so with sinners. We must receive the Spirit as a gift from Christ, who has kept the Law perfectly on behalf of the human race. Those who believe (receive) the truth concerning Christ's atoning death are endued with the Spirit as they assent to the Word of God.

For example, Acts 10:44 declares: "The Holy Spirit came on all who heard the message." From the time of Creation (Gen 1:2,3), the Spirit and the Word have worked together, and "therefore what God has joined together, let man not separate" (Mt 19:6).

Would you be filled with heaven's presence and power? Study, believe, and practice the Scriptures. This is the only way to victory for individuals and for the church as a whole.

A legend tells of a boy who was assured by a supernatural visitor, "Make a wish—any wish—and your wish shall be granted." The boy responded, "My one wish is that all my later wishes might also come to pass." A comparison of Matthew 7:11 and Luke 11:13 shows that the gift of the Spirit is the richest treasure of heaven bringing all other treasures in its train.

Are we surprised at the riches of the grace of God who confers upon us one unspeakable gift after another? He has given us his Son as our substitute and representative. And he has given us his Spirit as our advocate and comforter. All who accept Christ have the Son of God as their righteousness in heaven, and the Spirit as the continual presence of God beside them on earth, sufficient for every situation.

True, in our day, unbelief in Scripture has deafened the ears of most people to the gospel. But when the Word is made flesh in us—when like John the Baptist, in the spirit and power of Elijah, we live and move and have our being—then many will stop, look, and wonder. There are simple things that can be said, which for honest people can lead to faith in Scripture and their ultimate reception of God's priceless gifts of his Son and his Spirit.

Ask unbelievers why they think it is that human beings alone of all creation get bored. Horses and dogs and elephants do not get bored. Humans do. Why? Because, "He has set eternity in their hearts" (Eccles 3:11). We were made for God and will ever be restless until we rest in him.

Second, let us remind our friends that the human mind is the most complicated marvel in the whole universe. How is it that we have this computer on our shoulders that makes sense to us of all around us? The brain makes thousands of decisions every second (unconsciously to us) for it is in contact with every part of the body. Why is it that some inexplicable agitation of a little nervous tissue makes everything else possible? Most people use their minds as they use a window, without recognizing its presence. But it is a marvellous testimony to our Creator.

Third, to their surprise, remind those who doubt that the very existence of evil also points to the Creator of that moral law by which we recognize all that is wrong and that which is right. If there was no moral law we would take all evil for granted. Tell them also that the real mystery of existence is not the fact of evil, but the pervasive presence of good. What if all food tasted like dirt, and everything we saw looked grey? Suppose no one could smile, and no one could love. The greatest mystery to the unbeliever should be the existence of so many wonderful things. He can believe with Stephen Jay Gould that we are merely the result of about fifty billion coincidences, but does daily experience confirm this, or does it suggest something much more orderly and gracious?

Fourth, confront the doubter with Christ. He is the only person who has ever lived who foretold his enduring influence through all the endless aeons of eternity. "Heaven and earth will pass away, but my words will never pass away" (Mt 24:35). Suns and galaxies would wax old and die, but the words of the Galilean peasant would endure. How did he know?

Finally, tell out the wonders of the gospel, not least of which is the pledge of the indwelling Spirit of God for all who receive Christ.

When the Holy Spirit came down at Pentecost (Acts 2) he did not later return to heaven. He is still here waiting for surrendered temples to fill and use. He is the *Paraclete*—the one called alongside to help. No Christian need ever feel inadequate or afraid when he or she understands the meaning and blessing of Christ's supreme gift after Calvary. We have as much of the Spirit as we have of the Word of God understood and obeyed. Compare Ephesians 5:18 and Colossians 3:16. As soon as we surrender to the Gospel the Spirit comes. But make sure He is President and not just Resident. See Ephesians 1:13,14.

Chapter Nine:

The Elijah Message for the World

The last proclamation by the church (not a denomination, but the church of the twice-born) will issue a challenge like that of Elijah—a challenge to worship the Creator, not the idols urged by Antichrist. We have important hints as to the nature of the last proclamation and challenge in the New and Old Testament references to God's great prophet.

Both Testaments stress the unusual appearance of God's messengers. In 1 Kings 18 and the accounts of John the Baptist in the Gospels we are assured that those selected by Heaven to warn men give evidence that they are free of the glitter and glamour of the great of this world. Revelation 11 stresses that the clothing is sackcloth—symbolical emphasis on repentance, humility, and servanthood.

We are told that the first Elijah attended to God's altar and the Two Witnesses (the antitypical Elijah) do the same. See 1 Kings 18:30 and Revelation 11:1. Altars have to do with sacrifice and the shedding of blood. Our Lord's words at the Last Supper—"This is my blood of the new covenant, which is shed for many for the remission of sins"

(Mt 26:28, NKJV)—confirm that Christ's true followers see the pre-eminence of Calvary. Their loud cry to the world will demand attention to the Atonement.

Why is it that hitherto most have not responded to God's sacrificial love? Why have the majority of all nations not flocked to the gospel? The answer is very simple, but tremendously important. The majority reject the gospel because they think it is a demand, an imperious demand that will be costly to obey.

Matthew 22 with its story of the great Supper, and the unbelievable neglect of such a delectable invitation to feasting, makes this very clear. Consider the record:

> Jesus spoke to them again in parables, saying: "The kingdom of heaven is like a king who prepared a wedding banquet for his son. He sent his servants to those who had been invited to the banquet to tell them to come, but they refused to come."
>
> Then he sent some more servants and said, "Tell those who have been invited that I have prepared my dinner: My oxen and fattened cattle have been butchered, and everything is ready. Come to the wedding banquet."
>
> But they paid no attention and went off—one to his field, another to his business. The rest seized his servants, mistreated them and killed them. The king was enraged. He sent his army and destroyed those murderers and burned their city.
>
> Matt 22:1-7

Obviously this could never happen. People do not kill those who offer them a wonderful invitation. And those who do not accept an invite do not thereby become liable to execution. The hyperbole is deliberate so that we might see the magnitude of the folly of those who refuse the gospel invitation. It is the worst insanity and a colossal insult to Heaven.

Your salvation and mine could depend on our understanding of this parable. The gospel is not primarily a commandment to be obeyed, but an offer to be embraced. What we have here is not a demand being dodged, but a gift being declined. Here is not a failure to fulfil some austere duty, but a party being missed.

God is offering all something unbelievably good. He issues a call to a Homecoming with its deep joy and unceasing jubilation. It is a call to liberty and fruitfulness. Most people will be lost because of the priority they have given to secondary things. How frightening! Not deliberate wickedness, but inattention to what is best will destroy multitudes. We must remember that God either matters tremendously, or he does not matter at all.

Despite a million sermons to the contrary, the Gospel is not good advice! It is good news! Advice is something I should do, but news concerns something already done, and done by someone else. The Gospel is the good news that all God requires of me for time and eternity, has already been achieved by himself in the person of his Son, and that this achievement is credited to anyone, however vile, who believes the news.

Not all have recognized the exact date and place of their death. Three o'clock, Black Friday, Calvary. Christ represented the whole human race, and when he died, legally the whole world died. We were ruined ages before, without our participation, by the first Adam, our original Representative. At Calvary, again without our personal participation, we were redeemed by the second Adam, who represented us all. He was made what he was not, that we might be made what we are not. Despite our sin and selfishness, there is no need for us to try and reconcile God. He is already reconciled and beseeches us, "Be ye reconciled." God is offering something—not demanding something.

My standing before God depends on my acceptance of what Christ has done, not on what I am doing. For though the Law represents a perfect standard, it is powerless to impart to us a perfect standing.

> The believer is not called upon to make his peace with God: he never has or ever can do this. He is to accept Christ as his peace, for with Christ is God and peace. … You need not be anxious about what God thinks of you, but only what God thinks of Christ your substitute … Are you thinking that you must be free from sin before you trust his power to save? … Come to Jesus, and receive rest and peace. … Jesus loves to have us come to him, just as we are—sinful, helpless, dependent.
>
> Ellen G. White, *Selected Messages*, Vol., pp. 395, 351, 353

There are two aspects of Christ's work—the first is that which he did for us—which brings complete acceptance by God. This is complete and is never less at any stage of the Christian's experience. We do not fall from grace because we err. A million stumblings on the road to the New Jerusalem fail to bring the slightest whit of condemnation. But sanctification, Christ's second work (a work done not for us but in us), is never complete in this life. While my standing before God depends on what Christ has done for me, and not that which he does in me, it is also true that the second work is evidence that I have received the first. Luther declared that the Christian is "always a sinner, always a penitent, and always right with God."

The divine plan involves our complete restoration from sin—from its guilt, its power, and its presence. Our acceptance of Calvary brings the first, our dependence upon the living Christ brings the second, and his return will accomplish the last. The work is his, though received by our faith. Objectively, Christ is all. Subjectively, faith is all.

Look back to the Cross—that brings the faith that justifies; look forward to the coming—that brings the hope that sanctifies; look upward to the throne—that brings the love that satisfies. Good news indeed!

Drawing now from the New Testament, let us spell out the practical implications of this everlasting gospel. The more we behold Christ's perfect embodiment of infinite love and truth exemplified in his every motive, thought, look, word, and deed, the more our conscience would be vexed, did we not also believe that his personal righteousness is imputed every moment to foolish, erring, weak, stumbling believers. Similarly, the more we perceive the depths of the sacred law which demands of us all that Christ did and was in his humanity, the more we would despair, did not Scripture assure us that all who have surrendered their lives to the Saviour are, "accepted in the beloved" (Eph 1:6, KJV), "complete in him" (Col 2:10, KJV), "cleansed from all unrighteousness" (1 Jn 1:9), and without "condemnation" (Rom 8:1), or "separation" (Rom 8:33-39).

Despite the fact that we strive to fulfil every known duty, we remain "unprofitable servants" (Lu 17:10, KJV), righteous only by faith in the merits of Christ (Rom 3:20-26), "for we all make many mistakes" (Jas 3:2, RSV), and must pray daily, "forgive us our debts" (Mt 6:12).

Note that the continual ascending of the incense in Revelation 8:1-4 symbolizes the mingling of Christ's merits with our prayers, necessary because of the constant commission of sin. Simultaneously, we will rejoice that "Christ … is made unto us wisdom, and righteousness, and sanctification, and redemption" (1 Cor 1:30,31, KJV; and Zech 3:3,4), and that we can never be lost while trusting in his merits.

Furthermore, while sin remains in us and ever readily besets us, it shall not reign, for once we learn that our standing before God is determined by divine grace, "regardless of our success in keeping the law" (Rom 3:28, NEB), then sin ceases to have dominion over us (Rom 6:14). The tenor of our life is heavenward, despite manifold inconsistencies and failures. Being now united with Christ by faith, the fruit of righteousness is spontaneous (Rom 7:4). For it is not possible for us to accept Christ's death, without also accepting his resurrection life (Rom 6:1-12).

Paul declares that the two substitutes for the true gospel (lawlessness and legalism) are impossible for the true believer. Against lawlessness see Romans 3:31; 6:1-3,15; and 7:7. Against legalism see Romans 3:19-22 and 10:4, and Galatians 3:21,22. We cannot accept the work of the second member of the Godhead and reject that of the third (Gal 3:14). God gives his gifts with both hands, and justifies no man whom he does not proceed to sanctify. Paul's Epistles always present the finished work of Christ and then proceed to beseech the believer to make real in his or her life what they already have in Christ. Thus the latter half of the Epistles begin with "therefore," and appeal to holiness on the basis of the Atonement (Rom 12:1; Gal 5:1; Eph 4:1; Phil 4:1; and Col 3:1).

There will be no separation between justification and sanctification in our experience, but there will be distinction, for the first is complete and perfect, but the latter being the work of a lifetime, is neither complete nor perfect. For example, Christ's work is finished (Jn 19:30), and we have sat down in heavenly place with him (Eph 2:6). Yet, while the believer in Christ is viewed as already arrived, already "complete in him" (Col 2:10,12,13), there is still a struggle going on in the believer's experience (1 Cor 9:27; Gal 5:17; and Rom 7:14-25), showing that the believer comes short of God's glory (Rom 3:23), and needs forgiveness (1 John 1:8), until the return of Christ (Rom 8:23).

Thus in every place where Paul mentions, "the righteousness which is of faith," he means not sanctification, but that justification which is based on the finished atonement. Justification means a declaring righteous, never a making righteous—except legally—(Rom 1:16,17; 3:21,22,24; 4:5,11,13; 5:17,18; 9:30; and 10:13; Gal 5:6; and Phil 3:9). For justification is both instantaneous, one hundred percent (and outside of me); but it is not so with character development. The imputation of righteousness in justification is not a legal fiction, for when Christ died as the representative of the race, then "all died" (2 Cor 5:14); and when he rose, all rose (Col 3:1; and Eph 2:6). God declares us not subjectively righteous, but forensically so. Justification has to do with our standing before God, not our state or present condition. (Always remember that in the original Greek, "righteousness" and "justification" are the same word—thus justification by faith *is* righteousness by faith—not justification plus sanctification.)

Believing the good news, that our acceptance with Christ is conditioned on his perfection and not ours, we are free to work for others without feeling hypocritical concerning our inadequacies and failures. Only this gospel offers a message for others that will inspire faith, hope, and love, thus bringing that quality of life which all perfectionism strives in vain to accomplish. Is not this the approach of the New Testament, which, while sketching the many infirmities of the early believers, encourages them to fight the fight of faith with the assurance of an ultimate abundant entrance into heaven?

The New Testament offers many verbal pictures of the gospel that characterize the new age ushered in by the Cross of Christ. These figures include ransom, reconciliation, atonement, justification, propitiation, expiation, etc. The reality always transcends the figure, and the forensic understanding of justification does not imply that acceptance with God is merely a bookkeeping transaction. The gift of the indwelling Spirit and the event of regeneration ever accompany saving faith. But the forensic metaphor is invaluable for enabling those aware of their pollution of soul (Isa 6:5-7) to depend upon a perfect righteousness which was wrought out 2,000 years ago and offered today as a free gift immediately available to all who will accept it. This outward and upward look accomplishes a thousandfold more than all sanctified spiritual navel-watching could, for it lays the glory of man in the dust, and does for him what he can never do for himself. The Spirit of holiness does not speak of himself but testifies of Christ alone and his righteousness (Jn 15:26), and so should we. This everlasting gospel (Rev 14:6), the faith once-for-all "entrusted to the saints" (Jude 3) is the theme which has inspired all great revivals and should ever pervade Christian preaching (Gal 6:14; 1 Cor 2:2; and 1 Cor 15:3, RSV), swallowing up all other themes for it is the sweetest melody of human lips, the last hope for a hopeless world (Mt 24:14). Far from being a new-fangled heresy, it is the very gospel foretold in Genesis 3:15 and cherished by prophets, apostles, martyrs, reformers, and the greatest evangelists of all ages.

CHAPTER TEN:

GOD'S FIRE OR JEZEBEL'S?
THE TRUE OR THE COUNTERFEIT GOSPEL?

Despite all the divisions within Christendom and paganism, there are really only two religions in the world.

From the time of Adam's sin, all false religion has sought to clothe its nakedness by its own works in order to meet the requirement of a holy God. But true religion comes to God as an empty-handed beggar bringing only that which God himself has provided—the Lamb.

False religion has ever said: "Be good and God will love you." On the other hand, those who have discovered true religion echo Scripture's words, "This man receives sinners" (Lu 15:2, NKJV), God "justifies the ungodly" (Rom 4:5, NKJV), and Christ "has gone in to be the guest with a man who is a sinner" (Lu 19:7, NKJV).

While false religion makes the creature and his works central, true religion makes the Creator and his works the heart of everything. Thus we see the Jews coming to Christ and asking, "What shall we do that we might work the works of God?" Jesus replies: "This is the work of God that you believe on him whom he has sent" (Jn 6:28,29). The Pharisees

84

emphasized what they should do, but Christ put his emphasis on what God has already done in sending him, the Redeemer.

Why was the Cross needed if men could save themselves by their own works?

False religion majors in law and minors in love. True religion majors in love, and minors in law. The first majors in what God requires of us, and the second in what God has done for us. One religion puts all its stress on Christ as our example, the other on Christ as our substitute. One is a religion that leads to bondage, despair, and death. The other leads to joy, freedom, and life everlasting.

Saul, the Pharisee, belonged to the first religion, and as to the righteousness of the law he was blameless (Phil 3:6). But Paul the Apostle belonged to the second religion and he wrote, "I through the law died to the law that I might live to God" (Gal 2:19, NKJV; Rom 7:4). Paul knew that law was the foundation, the pillar and bulwark of the universe and as sacred as God himself. Nevertheless the Law is powerless to save the sinner. Thus the Apostle condemns law as a method of salvation, but exalts it as a standard. In Galatians 5:4, ASV, Paul wrote, "Ye are severed from Christ, ye who would be justified by the law; ye have fallen away from grace."

"Higher than the highest human thought can reach is God's ideal for his children." If no human thought can reach God's ideal, then what about our actions? Climbing up to heaven by Sinai is a risky business. One slip and we are done for. The Law demands a perfect nature, perfect motives, perfect feelings, perfect thoughts, perfect words, and perfect actions. It requires that every motive, feeling, thought, word and act be the best possible at every moment of time. No wonder that when Paul looked into the Decalogue in the light of Calvary he said, "I died" (Rom 7:7-14).

To break the Law just once brings not only guilt but also incapacity. Because of Adam's fall, from the very first moment of volitional living, we are guilty of selfishness, impurity, vanity, pride, and hatred. We have marred our nature and deserve death. The slightest sin is an infinite sin, for it is done against God who is an infinite being.

A religion of law always fails, because law cannot motivate sufficiently or forgive at all. The New Testament repeatedly contrasts law and grace, works and faith. Paul says about salvation, "If it is by grace, it is no longer on the basis of works; otherwise grace would no longer be grace" (Rom 11:6, NASB).

Paul's name heads 14 Epistles and every one of them is closed with a prayer for grace. Paul calls it "the free gift of God." Thousands have been kept out of the kingdom of God because they have not realized that salvation is a gift. Many today think they must do something to merit salvation. See what Paul says was the fatal error of his countrymen (Rom 9:31-32; and 10:3,4).

The law says, "This do and you will live." But grace declares, "Live and you will do." The law says, "Pay me what thou owest" but grace says, "I frankly forgive you all." The law says, "The wages of sin is death," but grace replies, "The gift of God is eternal life" The law says, "The soul that sins, it shall die," but grace "Whosoever believes has eternal life." The law says, "Make you a new heart," but grace, "A new heart will I give you." The law says, "Cursed is everyone that does not continue to do all the things written in the law," but grace, "Blessed is he whose sin is forgiven, whose transgression is covered." The law says, "You must love the Lord with all your heart, mind, and strength," but grace says, "Herein is love, not that we loved God, but that he loved us."

When the Law was given at Mount Sinai, 3,000 people died in a matter of days. When the gospel was proclaimed at Pentecost, 3,000 were given new life. 3,000 sermons on the Law alone will not convert one person. One sermon on the gospel can convert thousands!

The Law can only be truly obeyed when the heart is filled with the love of Jesus Christ in response to his love for us.

No one can obey God without loving him, and no one can love God until convinced that God has first loved him. The thief on the Cross had been put through plenty of law, but the law had not helped him. When he saw love incarnate, he was saved eternally.

To run and work, the law commands,

But gives me neither feet nor hands,

Better news the Gospel brings,

It bids me fly, and gives me wings.

The Bible designates all false religion as "Babylon." Jezebel, in chapter 2 of Revelation and in her portrayal in chapters 17 and 18 provides a description of meretricious religion with its idolatrous emphasis on things, and its character of pride and voluptuousness. In Genesis 11:4 we read of the first builders of old Babylon (Babel). They wished by their own efforts to reach heaven and make a name for themselves. They failed in both. Their type of religion brought heaven too low and made man too tall. All false religions use the same materials—mud and slime. Apart from God that's all we are. Animated mud.

On the other hand Jacob in the same book, is an example of true religion. He was a twister—that is what his name means. When his conscience smote him as God wrestled with him, he confessed that he was a rotter and a twister, a moral weakling, and then God gave him a new name and a new standing. Earlier in a dream he had seen a great ladder joining heaven to earth, with angels of God ascending and descending. This was the opposite of the Tower of Babel. God made the connection. The connection was the ladder interpreted by John chapter 1 as Christ. No wonder Jacob exclaimed: "This is the gate of heaven. This is the house of God," (Gen 28:17). Christ is the Gate, the Way and he is the Temple (house) of God. Jacob discovered that God was nearer than he thought. True religion teaches that God is very near penitent sinners—"nearer than breathing and closer than hands and feet."

On the Cross Christ represented every one of us. The frame of the Cross was the table on which he wrote our biography. His flesh was the parchment, the nails the quill, and his blood was the ink. His crucified hands and feet, his pierced brow and side, and thong-ribboned back tell the story of our life. Our feet have led us astray, and we have used our hands and minds selfishly. We have borne petty idols and loved foolish temporary things. His naked body reminds us that we do not have a stitch of righteousness to offer God.

The Cross is the real tree of the knowledge of good and evil. There we see our sinfulness, but also the love of God. Man was lost by partaking of the first tree of knowledge in Eden. Satan said "Take, eat," and man did so. Now Jesus says the same, as he stands by his Cross, offering us the merits of his sacrificed life. We are saved in the same way as we were lost—by taking and eating.

The Atonement is not just one doctrine within a body of Christian beliefs. It is the lifeblood running through the whole. Every important truth is presupposed by the Atonement, either included in it, or arising from it. Every imperative to practical godliness flows out of Calvary.

The good news is that our sins were crucified with Christ, nailed to his cross and then buried in Joseph's new tomb. Therefore the Law has no more power to condemn us than it can condemn Christ. If we do not see our complete death in him, sin will reign in us. No sin can be crucified either in heart or behavior unless it has first been pardoned in conscience through the precious blood of Christ. When the guilt of sin is not removed, the power of sin cannot be subdued (Rom 6:14). The Gospel announces that all men and women were legally justified at the Cross. "Whosoever will" may accept it and be saved.

Now we can understand those mysterious sections of the gospel narrative that tell us of the intensity of Christ's anguish when he sweat great drops of blood and later cried, "My God, my God, why hast thou forsaken me?" It is not the fear of death that explains Christ's agony. It was the awareness that he was suffering for the sins of the human race. He was forsaken of God, or so it seemed, that we might never be. He cried "Why?" in order that we might never be forced to utter that word.

The lightning bolts of justice struck the innocent Son of God in order that the guilty might find safety at the seared site of Calvary. It was no travesty of justice. The immutable law of God was more honored by the expiatory death of the infinite Son than if the whole human race had kept it perfectly. It was necessary that God, too, be justified. See Romans 3:26. There are more references in Scripture to the holiness of God than even his love, and unless it was demonstrated that sin was no light thing, that it deserved eternal death, the offer of forgiveness could only be a charade.

The one who receives the blood-bought gift of righteousness cannot remain the same. Looking to Christ justifies; gazing at Christ sanctifies. The amnesty given to the rebel dissolves the spirit of rebellion. See 1 John 4:17; and John 5:24.

I hear the words of love

I gaze upon the blood

I see the mighty sacrifice

And I have peace with God.

We are saved by grace alone, through faith alone, because of the blood alone. But the faith that saves is never really alone. We are not saved by faith plus works, but by a faith that works. Faith is not a doing but a seeing. It is also a hearing of the Gospel which enables us to see God's love for us and which begets faith in us. Faith is not a doing word, though it is a mighty active thing in the believer. Faith is a receiving word. It means to rest upon Christ's merits for time and eternity. To be saved by faith means to be saved *through* faith, not because of faith. For faith is the hand of a blind, starving, naked beggar accepting Christ's gift of clothing and bread.

I would not work my soul to save

For that the Lord has done,

But I would work like any slave,

For love of God's dear Son.

Chapter Eleven:
Can These Things Happen?

"Those who forget history are condemned to repeat it." Yes, these things shall be. They have already been in miniature many times. "That which is to be hath already been" (Eccles 3:15, KJV).

In the last 2,000 years, less than a few decades have been times of international quiet. Because the human heart is never at rest, and because passion so constantly agitates humans, wars inevitably erupt. From the seventeenth century to the present, war and revolution have been the tides engulfing most of the civilized world. Note the words of historian Kenneth Latourette when dealing with the French Revolution:

> The French Revolution was of major importance for the world. That was partly because it quickly had repercussions throughout most of Christendom, both in Europe and America. Paris, where the Revolution centered, was the most populous city of Western Europe and for a century or more France had been the most powerful realm in that region. So sweeping a series of changes could not fail to have effects of

primary importance in the rest of Western civilization. Of even more consequence was the fact that the French Revolution was an early and potent stage in a succession of similar movements which were to spread across the earth and which by the middle of the twentieth century were to alter profoundly the life of all mankind. The series began with the English Civil War, the Commonwealth, and "Glorious Revolution" of the seventeenth century, continued in the American Revolution of the 1770's and 1780's, came to an even more explosive phase in the French Revolution, went on with ever expanding geographic scope in Europe and the Americas in the nineteenth century, in the latter half of the nineteenth and in the twentieth century swept into Japan, China, and India, and through the Russian Revolution, and its aftermath profoundly molded much of mankind.

A History of Christianity, p. 1008

In our earlier chapters we have expounded those apocalyptic Scriptures that foretell that apostate religion, the religion of Jezebel with its idolatries and persecutions, shall ultimately dominate the world of the Last Days. But that domination will not be permanent, for the masses will rise and turn upon the pseudo-religion and destroy its protagonists. True Christians, threatened by the aggressive union of church and state, will yet see the greatest revolution of all time when earth in its chaotic woes will buckle under internecine conflict just prior to the return of Christ.

Such things have been before in miniature. For example, towards the end of the eighteenth century apostate religion dominated France, owning one fifth of the land, extorting tithes from the poverty-stricken peasantry, and growing fat by luxurious living while millions starved.

Then came the Revolution protesting against the state, which was nearly bankrupt because of its selfish indulging of an aristocracy that was as bad as the church. (Revelation 13 and 17 foretell a similar condition of church and state but on a worldwide scale.)

Nature intruded on the political and religious scene bringing the most severe winter known for almost a century. The crops had been decimated by floods, or frozen in the fields. Even the olive trees of Provence had died. In consequence there were about twenty million starving people and bread riots occurred everywhere. France was threatened with general anarchy, for even the soldiers (usually employed to put down riots) knew that a shotgun was no remedy for an empty stomach.

The reigning monarch futilely intervened but finally went to the guillotine and later so did his wife Marie Antoinette. Prior to that Austria and Prussia had decided to send their armies against France to save the king. Middle class leaders arose and tried desperately to stem the flood of troubles.

Carlyle wrote a famous book on the French Revolution. On one page we read:

> We are now, therefore, got to that black precipitous Abyss; whither all things have long been tending; where, having now arrived on the giddy verge, they hurl down, in confused ruin; headlong, pell-mell. Down, down;—till Sansculottism (the lower class Republicans) have [sic] consummated itself; and in this wondrous French Revolution, as in a Doomsday, a world have [sic] been rapidly, if not born again, yet destroyed and engulfed. Terror has long been terrible: but to the actors

themselves it has now become manifest that their appointed course is one of terror; and they say, Be it so.

The French Revolution, pp. 633

The "Reign of Terror" which succeeded failure after failure by the changing government bodies was the climax of mob violence which had in earlier years stormed and destroyed the Bastille, broken into the jails murdering the prisoners and reducing chateaux to ashes. Men and women seemed transformed into spirit-possessed wild beasts.

The Christian religion and its Sabbath were abolished. For a time the goddess of Reason was worshiped prior to the ascendency of Robespierre's deism. But the worst calamity was that described by *Encyclopedia Britannica* as follows:

The Law of Suspects empowered local revolutionary committees to arrest "those who by their conduct, relations or language spoken or written, have shown themselves partisans of tyranny or federalism and enemies of liberty." In 1793-94 well over 200,000 citizens were detained under this law; though most of them never stood trial, they languished in pestiferous jails, where an estimated 10,000 perished. About 17,000 death sentences were handed down by the military commissions and revolutionary tribunals of the Terror.

Vol 19:502, 15th edition

Let it not be thought that in our cultured, highly civilized era such things could never happen again. We have claimed in this volume that the Bible foretells a time of great tribulation such as has not been seen from the beginning of time. We have suggested that the time is coming when all men will be possessed either by the Spirit of God or the spirit of demons, and that in the last great day the tide of murderous multitudes will be arrested and then decimated by internecine strife. Have we forgotten that when Martin Luther King was assassinated there were riots in over 130 American cities? Have we forgotten the Holocaust and the SS murders of the cream of Poland's intelligentsia? (And lest we err by thinking that in World War 2, all the evils were perpetrated by one side alone, let us remember the scores of thousands of Germans who were incinerated by Allied bombs at a time when it was clear the war had been already essentially won.) And think of the innumerable parallel atrocities in our lifetime.

Also pertinent to our study is the fact that the French Revolution may not have occurred but for an earlier bloodbath which history knows as the massacre of Saint Bartholomew. On August 24, 1592, at the command of Catherine de Medici, Protestants were assassinated in their beds in Paris and throughout France—men, women, and children, murdered by the thousand. And it was the bells of a great church that gave the signal for the slaughter. In consequence the Huguenots, the cream of the country, fled from France. Had Protestantism been alive and well at the end of the eighteenth century, the French Revolution with its Reign of Terror may never have happened. So say some historians.

Shakespeare was the representative writer of the Elizabethan era. Dante and Goethe represented their eras, but the man who epitomizes in his writings the characteristic features of the 20th century is one unknown to most. His name was Franz Kafka, a Czech Jew, who died early of tuberculosis. Most people who knew him thought he had only written a few scraps for circulating among his intimates, but 40 years after his death in 1924, a partial list of his writings, their editions, and commentaries in 30 languages ran into over 400 pages.

The books of Kafka studied today include *The Trial, The Castle, The Penal Colony, America, The Metamorphosis*. Why are they so impressive?—because they offer an uncanny forecast of the crises of the later years, especially World War 2. One biographer writes:

> Kafka foresaw, in an act of clairvoyance more telling than explicit prophecy or political argument, the world of the death camps; he heard the knock of the faceless policemen on the night door; he saw human beings transmuted to vermin and swept into garbage. … It is in Kafka even more than in Marx that we find the controlling insight of our historical epoch—the absolute extension to man of the logic of mass production, the transformation of politics with their potential of anarchic challenge into the inertial, self perpetuating motion of technology.
>
> The waiting rooms in our anonymous hospitals, the punch cards on which our lives are programmed, the visas we hunger for in vain, the Chinese walls we have built across our cities, all these are Kafka scenarios. … We diminish before them to the stature of the "little man," of the harried monad whom Kafka and Chaplin have made our mirror.

George Steiner, *Brief Lives*, pp. 423-425

When John the Apostle was inspired to write Revelation he had in his mind the terrible persecutions of the monster Nero when Christians were dipped in tar and set alight as beacons in Nero's gardens. These prefigured what was to come on a worldwide scale.

We have not told a tithe of the record of history regarding Christian and other scapegoats. Russia's murders of Christians following the 1917 revolution and the later rule of Stalin alone would fill many large books. But perhaps this is enough to indicate that the biblical teaching of a great time of trouble ahead for the world and the church has already had many foreshadowings.

However, Christ says to each of us, "Be not afraid, only believe" (Mark 5:36). He still walks on the boiling sea in every storm, and all that threatens to come down on our heads is under his feet.

After he broke the bread and multiplied it for the 5,000 he went up to the mountaintop to pray. From there he saw his disciples in the dangerous waters toiling desperately and on the verge of drowning. But he came down from the mountain, walked on billows, and entered their boat. Immediately it was safely at the shore. There in that record of John chapter 6 we have 2,000 years of typified history of the church, including Christ's "breaking" on Calvary, his ascension to heaven and his heavenly ministry, and finally his return to his church to save them out of great tribulation—the Second Advent.

Alleluia!

Sursum Corda

Epilogue

In 1 Corinthians 10:6,11 we are told that the experiences of Israel are "types," i.e., paradigms of events significant for the New Testament era. (See the margin of verses 6,11 for referral to the Greek original.) Christians have long been aware of this important key to Scripture. "That which is to be hath already been" (Eccles 3:15, KJV).

From the very first chapter of Scripture to the end of Malachi, typology is prominent. For example, the creation story is a type of the new creation in Christ—redemption. See 2 Corinthians 5:17; Jn 1:1; 1 Pet 2:9. The first Adam, the head of the race, the image of God, whose side was opened on the sixth day that he might have a bride, pointed to Christ the Last Adam.

All the sacrifices described in Exodus and Leviticus point to Calvary, as did every priest and High Priest of Israel and their tabernacle and temple. Prophets, priests, and kings, events, and institutions testified to the coming Saviour and his work of atonement.

In the Bible's closing book we have over 500 references to the Old Testament, and it is quite impossible to interpret the Apocalypse without familiarity with the earlier Scriptures. There we are pointed to Israel's tabernacle and temple, her feasts and sacrifices, and her history.

Balaam, Jezebel, Elijah, Pharaoh and Egypt, the Red Sea, Sodom and Gomorrah, Babylon, Edom, Megiddo, etc., all reappear in Revelation.

Revelation chapters 1-11 set out the Church's history to the eve of the end-time, but chapters 11-22 are all about the end-time itself. In the first half we have seeds of what will be enlarged in the latter half. Balaam is a type of the false prophet of Revelation 13, and Jezebel whose work is similar typifies the great religious apostasy of the Last Days, a worldwide Jezebel whose leaders will unite under the antitypical Balaam (the false prophet) and the Beast (the primary Antichrist) led by the serpent Satan. Our first encounter with the beast was in Daniel chapters 7, 8, and 11.

This little book has endeavored to spell out the significance of the Old Testament types centered in Jezebel and Elijah as suggested by the book of Revelation. Both Testaments foretell a time of trouble worse than anything previously known in the history of the world. That time of trouble was typified in the days of Elijah and Jezebel. Christ admonished us in his sermon on the end of the world (the Olivet discourse) to understand what prophecy had foretold about that crisis (See Mt 24:15-31).

Our present world since 1945 with its nuclear detonations is a very fragile one. Politicians whisper to each other that if the masses knew just *how* fragile, there would be panic and anarchy. But those who know the gospel need not fear. They can lift up their heads knowing that their redemption draws nigh and with it the end of sorrow, pain, death and the curse. To understand the everlasting gospel is to be armed against whatever is coming on our globe. In these pages we have described that gospel and the final Pentecost, which will offer it to every nation, kindred, tongue, and people.

May you, too, rejoice in that "good, glad, and merry tidings, which makes the heart to sing and the feet to dance."